Whenever I read a poem by Kai Coggin, I feel something transcendent—her words resonate and reverberate within my soul. She keeps elevating us. A poem is a sacred place, a quiet agreement between the poet and the reader, the spoken word and the receiver—it is indeed holy. The hum in my chest from a moan, the flesh popping between the snaps in my fingers, my whole body moved through these poems. Kai is indeed a *Mother of Other Kingdoms* and while reading her offerings, I became a daughter of other moons, a spiritual tether bound to her poems, a line that will never break. "A mother is quietly building something out of nothing" . . . as most mothers do, and Kai's words build crescendos in my spirit, as I recall her lines singing through my daily life. Between each line there is a symphony of nature and resistance, the harmonizing tension and release of a poem. While reading I wept, celebrated, and met my curiosities with surrender to Kai's words—they are indeed holy. With so many beautiful moments to count—black snake, earthquake, fox, unicorn, hummingbird baptism, son flowers—it's a jungle of blessings. *Mother of Other Kingdoms* is both a blade of steel and of soft grass, piercing and bending my heart to remember to love myself and others in any way that I can. Kai is an archetype of poetic genius, and this book is her opus, truly a masterpiece. Kai's "heart is fertility itself," and I am a daughter/sister/ auntie to her verses. I am grateful for the reminder of how powerfully tender love can be. May we all mother and nurture the worlds around us. Asé.

CC Mercer Watson, author of *A Love Story Waiting to Happen*

Kai Coggin's gleaming collection of poems, *Mother of Other Kingdoms*, is a testament to the power of language to sing our hearts open "despite the world breaking at every line." Wide-ranging in its subject matter, this book explores urgent topical issues like race, ancestral trauma, and body image while also diving deeply into longing, nature, and love. More than anything, Coggin has written an ode to living this life, a life that is flawed the way a diamond is flawed, its inclusions unable to dim its bright beauty. In poem after poem, wild with love, she zooms in on our world and "consecrate[s] / the mundane / into / the sublime."

Francesca Bell, author of *What Small Sound*

Kai Coggin's *Mother of Other Kingdoms* is not only nurturing and healing, but reading this collection is akin to the practice of mindfulness needed in these troubled times. Her poems are handfuls of peace, moving rains over cracked earth—they hold us, sometimes on fragile branches, sometimes after an explosion, always with love. Coggin is one of our most treasured voices.

Edward Vidaurre, author of *By Throat, By Miracle: New & Selected Poems*

MOTHER
of OTHER
KINGDOMS

MOTHER
of OTHER
KINGDOMS

Kai Coggin

Harbor Editions
Small Harbor Publishing

Cover: *Kai and Genghis*, a painting by Joann Saraydarian 2024.
Author photo by Jeff Fuller-Freeman

MOTHER OF OTHER KINGDOMS
KAI COGGIN
ISBN 978-1-957248-22-6
Harbor Editions,
an imprint of Small Harbor Publishing

Contents

III.

IV.

V.

FOREWORD

"Can you see why I mother every possible thing?" Kai Coggin asks in *Mother of Other Kingdoms*. Here, in "Tender and Ache," the poet has scooped a bumble bee from the windowpane, cupped his slow body, and carried it to a lilac tree. "If you die, at least die happy inside here," the poet says to the bee. But the bee does not die—not yet anyway—and several hours later, Kai witnesses the bee buzzing by—"I'm alive!–" and tells us: "This is how I mother. I rock the smallest species to sleep, / lullaby our deepest human apologies into their innocent ears." It is this rocking of the smallest species—this profound attention to each and every soul in the world—which radiates from Kai's being.

Kai Coggin—Certified Master Naturalist, woman, advocate, wife, friend, lover, spirit, daughter, sister, auntie, editor, prize winner, inaugural Poet Laureate of the City of Hot Springs, host of the longest running consecutive weekly open mic series in the country—reminds us with each tender turn in her new book that at this moment, we are living. In poems built from a vulnerable attention—"to the holiness of the infinitesimal–" I find, over and over, what I need to be reminded of, not only to be a poet, but to be living in a body on this planet of "intersecting apocalypses."

I met Kai during my own personal apocalypse. Deep in the pandemic of 2020, scrolling through my infinite Facebook feed, I started seeing Kai hold her hand to the screen as she hosted her virtual Wednesday Night Poetry Open Mic. There were plenty of heavy hitters—Ada Limón on her screened-in porch, the post-storm birds chirping as she reads "The Conditional–" and "Say tomorrow doesn't come;" Naomi Shihab Nye's beautiful homage to her eccentric Aunt Hilda; Diane Seuss "starting in childhood and working her way out" as she shares from her Pulitzer Prize-winning *frank: sonnets*—but what felt most essential was the accumulation of voices for which Kai made space. I'd just been given a Stage 2 breast cancer diagnosis; I was terrified; I wrote a poem that I wanted to share. I knew immediately and with certainty I wanted to share it through the world Kai had created. For Kai, "all of [her] eyes are open;" her heart is open, her mind, her arms—if you're lucky enough to meet her in person—to envelop you in a hug.

And so yes, while I recognize this is an introduction to *Mother of Other Kingdoms*, I also know this is a bit of a song of love and appreciation for Kai and all she does in the poetry world—her ability to hold us all and to do so in the hardest of times—because, quite simply, I cannot separate the poet from the poems. Kai teaches me, over and over, in her poems and in her spirit, that to isolate one thing from another is to do a disservice to both. To be as supple and vulnerable as Kai is a wish I have for each and all of us. But it is not simply Kai's compassion towards all beings—green peppers and dill; prismatic rainbows and paralyzed spiders; queer kids and skywriting poets; light and toil; Alexander and Genghis; her mother and her wife—it is her ability to name and to see each of these beings in their complexity. Here, in the opening poem:

> And if we use our words
> to name it,
> to notice
> the unnoticed,
> and make it holy with poem—
> we consecrate
> the mundane
> into the sublime
>
> letter
> by letter,
> line
> by line.

There is, in fact, a holiness with which Kai approaches each poem and each subject, a refreshing unironic reverence which in itself deserves to be revered.

In "Crashing Toward Light," Kai situates us in the world as it is, "in the summer of fire in the year of drought in the age of unreasoning in a biosphere of bombing in an epoch of endless suffering—" and then asks, "what of this world is left for poems?" She flips on the switch and discovers a "giant triceratops beetle / ambling in the dark across [her] kitchen floor," and then tells us that these beetles are known to fly "with a force toward all that is bright and warm." It is Kai's deepest manifesto: to recognize darkness but to seek light. In that same poem, with a toothpick, Kai swirls off the tangled "cotton candy webs" of a spider from "his barbed leg" and "clean[s] him like he is [hers] before releasing him back into the wild night." This tender cleaning, this caretaking, this mothering of the natural world is central to Kai's work in the world.

And yet, as with all who mother, there is so much more than caretaking. There is the sexiness of "Talking Dirty" and "the long blue tie from the silk robe . . . all the times I pull her into me." There is the subtle humor of "Ode to Ramen Noodles," "as sacrament as surrogate." There is also the inevitable grief of knowing that to mother one thing comes at the expense of not being able to mother another. "Is there ever a threshold of tenderness?"

Kai asks in "Midwifing Tadpoles in the Anthropocene." "I never want to cross it," she answers.

What's essential, though, is the way Kai brings us to that threshold again and again, making an altar of tenderness itself. In "Catalog of Receiving," Kai beautifully bombards us with the gifts of the world. Perhaps the "You" of this poem is Kai's wife, Joann, but it also feels as if the "you" is the complicated swirl of everything around the speaker—*the morning, and mourning; broken glass and dewy grass; vex, and hex, and sex, and feeling beautiful naked finally*—the relentless gifts offered and, more importantly, Kai's unabating acceptance of those gifts. Kai understands that the gifts from the world are multiple. I'm thinking of the "box full of darkness" that Mary Oliver once received, how Kai would place that too on her altar of tenderness.

Kai begins *Mother of Other Kingdoms* with an epigraph from Adrienne Rich: "Without tenderness, we are in hell." This epigraph serves as a harbinger announcing tenderness is a choice—a choice for Rich, a choice for Kai, a necessary choice for all of us who do not wish to live in hell—and that chosen tenderness must extend to all beings and must also be turned inward to ourselves. Of all the beings that Kai mothers in this book, I am most moved by how she mothers her own inner child. "Look at our beautiful breaking world," Kai writes in "Do You Want to Play Outside?" "It gets so hard, doesn't it?" she asks. "We can still search out the wonder, can't we?" And then she takes her inner child "to the lip of the water / and show[s] her the colors of the golden slick bodies / glinting the light of morning in slants of sun," and she takes us and our own inner child with her. She continues:

> Maybe that's the answer, this small world, this ripple of influence,
> these beautiful circles in which we swim around
> feeling each others pains—
> maybe if we take each other's hands,
> if our inner children find each other again
>> before the maddening of adulthood,
>> before the cynicism of growth,
>> before the ache of aging,
> maybe if we just knocked on each other's doors and asked sincerely—

And, oh how vulnerable and sincere Kai is in her asking—*Hey, do you want to play outside with me?*—and all I can think is: yes, yes, Kai, I do.

Nicole Callihan

for JOANN, GENGHIS & LAYLA
my precious family

and for my more-than-human children with their elaborate taxonomies

"Without tenderness, we are in hell."

—Adrienne Rich

"If you see for yourself, hear for yourself,
and enter deeply enough this seeing and hearing,
all things will speak with and through you."

— Jane Hirshfield

" This is the first, wisest, and wildest thing I know: that the soul exists,
and that it is built entirely out of attentiveness."

"To live in this world, you must be able to do three things: to love what is mortal;
to hold it against your bones knowing your own life depends on it;
and when the time comes to let it go, to let it go."

—Mary Oliver

PRIEST OF THE INVISIBLE

"The poet is the priest of the invisible."
    —Wallace Stevens

It's like we walk around
with magnifying glass
over our eyes,
amplifiers tied
to our ears—
this close listen,
this peer into and hear
the infinitesimal movement of cells
reaching toward beauty,
reaching toward light.

And if we use our words
to name it,
to notice
the unnoticed,
and make it holy with poem—
we consecrate
the mundane
into
the sublime

letter
by letter,
line
by line.

I.

Coming to a Poem

I hear there are nine gates,
ten windows,
a winding road through a one horse town,
a night perhaps and all her stars,
the movement up and through an open heart
breaking
reshaping
into something whole.

But in these middle times,
between the *before* and perceived *after* times of this pandemic,
during this intersection of multiple apocalypses,
I come to my poems in the morning.

I wake up early,
before the two-legged and four-legged family I call mine.
I wander quiet through the sleeping house
and go outside where the wild and hungry ones wait for me—

cardinal, wren,
grosbeak and titmouse,
perched on yawning branches,
all sing an ethereal forest-alarm-rise-melody,
and I pour little mounds
of black sunflower seeds, nyjer, and thistle,
call them to breakfast with the silent sound of care.

Our beautifully fat koi fish swirl
in their golden-streaked sunrise pond,
wait for their handfuls of food,
dance infinities before me in a whirl of colors.
I greet them each by name—
Lion, Blue, Biggie Stardust, and Spirit,
my baby whales,
my children
of another kingdom.

Bumblebees and butterflies,
hummingbirds whirring—
our collective of winged creatures
cross their trajectories in the path of my grounded body,
and I fly inside myself as the sun moves above the horizon.

The green growing garden beds wait their turn—
they know
I am coming soon.
Rising light shines through morning leaves
creating patient fires that don't burn,
just warm me with graceful reaching.

I become a moving rain toward them,
shower the hibiscus gardenia chrysanthemum
coneflower salvia marigold rose and peony—
a whole catalog of blooming,
reciprocal nourishing
for early risers like me.

The vegetable garden is last to be soaked—
climbing cucumber and yellow crookneck squash,
tomatoes glowing like reddening planets,
eggplant jalapeño lettuce basil green peppers dill.
I make prismatic rainbows with the shower of water
pointed in certain slants of sunlight
and smile like I am a god
or some weather pattern of my own.

These moments of silence
at the start of the day—
this quiet wildness,
this tending and feed

      before the news of some everyday tragedy rocks me to the core
      some fire or flood or unnamed catastrophe of war

these moments hold me.

I walk through this open door,
creep outside our sleeping house
to where the wild and hungry things wait for me.

There are many ways to come to a poem—

I start here.

PETALS

this morning
I ache
to touch
you

outside
the   wind is cold   and rowdy
ripping   spring   buds
off   the   trees
with a degree of   wildness
that is reserved
            only for the natural

between seasons
it is your name
that holds
me

the ground is littered
with wind-swept petals

all I hear is *she loves me she loves me she loves me*

Knitting Sweaters for Hummingbirds

for Archilochus colubris

Can't talk! Knitting sweaters for the hummingbirds!

these words actually came out of her mouth
and she was joking around
in a rush of protecting every precious thing
before a spring freeze cold front
untimely blew in

but it's not far off
from how much she actually cares
for all our winged pawed and hoofed friends
who share our peaceful valley

it's not beyond imagination
compared to the close attention
she gives to the every-colored birds
plants flowers trees frogs fawns butterflies bees

every little life out there
that might secretly be voicing a need
it's like she hears them whispering to her
in a vibration I cannot even see

and while the snow falls
on a freak winter-clashing-spring day
I can picture
the jewel-ruby throats
of hummingbirds
safe and warm
protected
with the invisible
tiny tweed turtlenecks
her thoughts
knitted
in her dreams

HUNGERS

for Odocoileus virginianus

The mother doe and her fawn have been eating all my flowers.
I wake up to water a massacre of leaves,
guillotined color, hoof-prints left in moonlight.

I imagine the vibrant pink roses and hibiscus crunching in their teeth,
bursting bright hues, rich red dahlia petals
lining their long thick throats,
the playful zinnias sliding through
whatever curves deer intestines might wander like,
and mammoth sunflower heads blooming a thousand rising golden lights
in the underbellies of this deer mother, her daughter, still spotted with newness,
and I don't mind my flowers finding their masticating mouths,
this wild decadence I planted from seed
making way
to their hungers.

VERTIGO

I became a spinning planet last week
maybe after the red wine
but it surely stayed
overnight
into day   days   daze
this centripetal dance
toward the center of the galaxy
inside my own head
clutching
for the gravity
I once knew but had   lost
turning
            turning
                        (please stop) turning

how do I still this whirl-pooling vessel?

am I becoming a star?

my mouth black holes
my inner ear drums revolutions
I cannot fight
my eyes pirouette
in their scared sockets

vertigo
is a jarring float   out   of body
what is my soul doing   pulling   away?

this
disconnected
dizzy dizzy   dance   walking slant   spinning   oblivion   fall
while my body grabs for
the closest
thing
to
solid
ground
her thigh
her hands
the force that is stronger than spinning out of control   love.

MY GYM SELFIES TAUGHT ME

in facebook memories
these sweaty versions of my
heart-pumping former selves
glisten their persistent victories
shout like echoes from my round face
of how driven my body was
to lose
to lose
to lose
twenty thirty forty fifty sixty pounds
beast-moding the free weights
squatting the world's beauty standards
running on a treadmill for hours going nowhere
muscles defining new words for reflection
lunging forward into some other version of self

this self
        today
just twenty more pounds
short of what was once *the goal*

until the goal became
just don't die
        just don't catch it
            just wash your hands
                just wear a mask and bleach your groceries

just stay in your house
        with your love
            and her laughter
        with your dogs
            and their soft snores
        with your garden
            and all its gorgeous blooming

forget the gym—

just go within
and find the self that survives

the self who's been there all along
despite your size

Patrocenia and Imogene

a villanelle for my grandmothers

I am a granddaughter alive and unclaimed
        of grand maternal hearts Patrocenia and Imogene—
all I know of them is their names.

My longing for them, these words proclaim,
        Patrocenia, a buried seed on a rice farm in the Philippines—
I am a granddaughter alive and unclaimed.

A spirit within me rises fiery and untamed,
        my other matriarch, Irish orphan Imogene—
all I know of her is her name.

In sepia, her soft curls and round face fill a frame.
        Mothers of my parents with oceans lost between;
I am a granddaughter alive and unclaimed.

I imagine their wisdom, what cells make us the same,
        how each shaped their own lineage as someone's queen—
all I know of them is their names.

Within me there is a deep strength and a burning flame,
        ancestral atoms swirl inside with a knowingness unseen—
I am a granddaughter alive and unclaimed.

All I know of them is their names.

SHORELESS IN ASIA

after Ilya Kaminsky

I left a country I have since forgotten and another country that never held me as its own child. Two countries, like a forked tongue in a muted mouth. Two shores that slip away at every step toward, sand un-becoming, an oceaning underfoot. Only two words of those distant lands hold my cheekbone to the ground to listen. They whisper in erasure. Awash.

บิดา: Thai for Father, birthplace language, where you were once mine. American journalist in Thailand, CIA spy, man with two families, undercover, body-double dad, and yet—a solid tree whose thigh I clutched onto the moment before you left, before you left us in your America without you, a tall tree of leaving, my hands gripped to your pant leg in desperate remember, deciduous, falling away, completely.

> บิดา, Dad, you are twelve years dead now. I whisper your fleeting names into the wind to meet the scattered ashes of your many faces. I meet my own face there. I'm a writer now, Dad. Are you proud?

Bahay: Tagalog for home, another land, caribou tracks in Calibungan fields and fields of rice, *sakahan* meaning farm, the family farm, sun on my uncles' dark faces, flip-flopped feet, the smell of wet grain, a pig roasting over fire, *de la Cruz* surname uncrossed, flies and laughing and heat, mother tongue which I do not speak, my mother land, land of my mother. She calls me *anak*, and I cry in another language. I taste home with an American mouth, traded *bahay* for assimilation.

> *Nanay*, Mother, you gave up the Philippines for this American Dream—we chased it, and we caught it in our teeth. We were lost children together, all of us. I am older now than you were then, and still I am many nights a child. You and your two daughters—three small foreigners in a land we never knew until we called it home, with everything lost. With everything yet to lose.

CLUTCH

after Diane Seuss

I drive to a playground and just listen to them laugh,
watch as they spark conversations with each other, melt inside
at imagination leading and questions not far behind. They glow outside
of me, and my womb is an empty field of bleeding hearts.
If there is truly the taste of regret stirred into this poem, it is warm milk
leaking from my full breast into nothing's mouth. It is my arms formed
into cradle, rocking no one back and forth, my lips mouthing silent
songs, lullabying goodbyes to who was never born into hello.
I drive to a playground, walk toward the whimsy of their day,
sit on a small rusted horse on a fat metal spring, and sway like a ghost.
This is the lonely road of regret that leads to the grass underfoot of ache,
the sigh of tomorrows empty of growing, the cycles of my uncreated children
still sitting somewhere as stardust, hovering over me, waiting
for the clutch of my hand to break through the sky.

A Star with My Brown Eyes

I have imagined the rooms inside myself—
four chambers in which you can hide your toys,
clothes you will outgrow,
shoes I will bronze with affection.
You are but a starlight glow, shimmering with possibility,
and I am down here with my feet dug deeply into the earth,
weaving a womb for you of gossamer and twilight,
a soft place for all the tenderness of you to land,
a homecoming for the you-niverse to take shape in my cellular division.

I would divide myself into microscopic infinitudes
in order to build you up,
in order to create space for you to form
from the invisible into the tangible
> touch
> suckling mouth
> tiny fingers
> divine warmth.
I am waiting
child,
my dear child.
I would give you the eternal home of my patient chest,
the supple orchard I have finally garnered
worthy of your sweet becoming.
Are you coming?

I may never push you out.

I may always want to be the fortress around your glowing heart,
the shelter keeping treasure safe, the mother
who builds walls of her own flesh to protect you.

I know, too, I have warrior genes—
that the one I choose to manifest you from stardust
will serve only the purpose of this predestined conception,
immaculate in its design, aligned with a promise I made to the sun.

I know my blood is an ancient mix.
There is nothing ordinary about this labor,
the long waiting

until the time comes when you appear,
a mirror of my heart,
a bloom of the infinity inside me.

Your spark of life—
pulled
from the cosmos
   into matter
   into earthen-form
   into a body of flesh and bone
will already be my hero
will already be my triumph and salvation.

Will the constellation I have swallowed
turn outward, here?

I am a mother without a child,
my body is a warehouse of shelved daydreams,

prayers   and blueprints   and lullabies
line the lining of my womb
and somewhere
a star with my brown eyes
is falling
slowly
to
the
earth.

UNDER THE TABLE

My first boyfriend was in 5th grade, I guess.
Rene Luna—luna like moon,
like a dead planet, cold and empty,
but at eleven, I thought I would try boys
before totally committing my life
to the love of women,
their softness,
and he was left handed, so we held hands
in social studies under the table.
I never even kissed him once.
My best friend Carmen and his best friend Mark
were a couple, too, so it was a thing—
this puppy love, more like puppy lost,
and did I mention I never kissed him,
and Carmen and Mark were probably
running all the bases by that time,
while I hid in the batter's box
swinging at shadows,
and I wouldn't say
my first and only boyfriend ever
was anything close to love,
but more like a test drive
of a car you know you don't want,
this old clunker of a thing,
and you take it for a spin just to see
the steering is all wrong
and there's a weird smell,
but he was a nice kid,
and we held hands in social studies,
under the table,
his right hand in my left,
both of us diligently keeping our pencils moving
so our teacher Mr. Saenz wouldn't see,
under the table,
secret,
so no one else would see,

especially Kelly Nelzeen
whose blonde hair was so pretty.

WAITING FOR A STORM

It is windy inside the house,
and if I know anything, it's this—
you are always waiting for a storm, you are kissing the breeze out loud
with the words of a story that has been locked inside your chest for centuries,
opened treasure finding its way to now,
the bellows of our house singing a song of release into the night air.

It is windy inside the house,
and I have always been one to hide from the rain,
you dance naked in it like a baptism,
like all of your sins were borrowed so you could feel
the freedom in their washing away,
give them back to the earth,
for you are made of cosmos and diamonds,
you bend light into rainbows with your violet hands.

It is windy inside the house,
every moment is an adventure with you,
like nothing is impossible and there is a mountain
we have already climbed if we just look down,
but the constellations above are too much like sisters
for us to care about what's under our feet,
let's keep dancing like this for hours,
in this symmetry of movement we call our bodies.

It is windy inside the house,
we have turned out all the lights
and candles lantern our space in the wild,
the storm has passed with barely a drop,
but the lightning in my heart for you
is answered with the thunder of your voice
a second later, the storm is here.

The storm is us.

Living Room Fire Tent

I remember the ice storm we had that first Christmas in Arkansas
when the sky fell in frozen sheets, and power lines bowed
with the bending curves of the thin pines, and the snapping of both
brought a white-out-black-out that lasted days, maybe weeks.

It was freezing, 19 degrees I think.

We played like children in the snow all day,
snowball fights, snow angels, and sledding down the steep hills of our land,
whizzing around naked maples and oaks on a metal bowled tray,
sleek slalom of doom and laughter and crashing.
I remember how the silent snow-covered tree trunk
sent me   tumbling off   the   slick   track,
unintentional olympian flipping through the air with a landing
that did not impress the (squirrel) judges.
The butts and knees of our jeans turned from wet to crackling ice,
the sounds of our laughter cut the frozen air,
and our patient house slowly let out the belly of her warmth
as each hour passed in her snowed-in seclusion.

All the firewood was wet turned icicle,
unprepared stacks of logs left outside turned igloo,
turned snow castle, turned winter wonderland of wasted warmth.
The fireplace howled the cold emptiness of wind
blowing through our chimney,
and frost painted white stars on the windows.

We drove to the grocery store. The whole town was shut down
and the night manager was locking up the closed store
when we walked up to the door pleading for some dry firewood,
the pallet of bagged logs stacked high just inside,
our frozen fingers knocking on the breath-fogged glass
with the desperation of a Dickens novel.

It was the first lesson on learning
the meaning of *neighbor* in this Valley of the Vapors,
the first sign that people here in Hot Springs have such heart.
He slid open the glass doors
carrying huge armfuls of dry wood out to us,
went back inside and grabbed even more.

He loaded up our jeep with heat to warm us for days, wouldn't take our money.
Our gratitude created a circle of warmth around the parking lot,
and the snow was beautiful as it fell.

When we got home, we pulled the couch up close to the fireplace,
we built a raging fire, and the house exhaled our relief.
You used bamboo and canvas painters drop-cloths
to build us a tent around the couch and fire,
and we shrunk the size of our home
to huddle around the the heat of the hearth—
my heart always warmer next to you.

The ice storm white Christmas all those years ago is like a beautiful dream,
a snow globe fantasy sitting quietly on the bookshelf of my heart,
there for me to hold in my hands when beauty seems out of reach,
when the world grows colder, darker, colder, darker still.

The power restored just when the romance and novelty
of the situation started to melt like the snow,
but I'll hold onto the glowing memory for warmth.

I'll remember those quiet winter days circling a hearth
in a bamboo and canvas fire tent inside our snow-covered house,
with you and our little dogs, and the bending pines outside,
bowing their noble necks to peek in through our windows,
to witness what love and home
really look like.

II.

BIRDWATCHING

they should just call it stillness
absolute stillness and lots of waiting
absolute waiting and not moving
not moving really at all
so try to blend in
wear clothes that fade into the background
hide among bushes and behind the arms of low trees

statue yourself
act *natural*
merge with it all
find peace within yourself
I know it sounds new-age but it's true
quiet your always-turning-churning mind
find calm
find motionless
sway if the trees are swaying though
move slightly with the breeze if it blows

vibrate on *their* wavelength
not yours

have your camera ready
poised so that you do not have to lift it up to your eye
propped so that your arms are resting on something
balcony railing
window sill
branch
knee
so that you don't have to move too much
when a bright wonder ever-so-briefly flies into your frame

account for wing-speed
hummingbirds will take an adjustment to un-blur the whirr of their hover
enjoy the vibrant displays of cardinal indigo bunting grosbeak goldfinch oriole
the sparrows titmouse and doves too are beautiful

one in every few dozen photographs will be perfect
the others are just dances
that have nothing to do with you

KEYS

If you listen really close, my dog can say *hello*.
He isn't showy about it, but the intonations of his mouth
can shape into conversation, I swear.
I ask him where the keys are and he says *I don't know*
but isn't that the key anyway? Asking? Listening?

I like research and answers, have a jeopardy mind,
a numbers game, no abstractions, concrete, just the facts, ma'am.

The tallest tree in the world is a coastal redwood named Hyperion, and he hides
in California's redwood forest, only a few scientists can pinpoint his location.
Sequoia sempervirens, more than two Statues of Liberty tall.
Let's put our country's fading torch in his 380-foot treetop.
Our liberties are shrinking and already the world
does not recognize our shores.
Hyperion, clouds sweep your limbs and kiss your bright green face.
Take a deep breath, gentle giant, your secret is safe.
We know you stand for other things besides our exaggerated grandeur.

I like to look at the wonder of it all—like did you know
that 70% of the white sand on Caribbean
and Hawaiian beaches is made from the poop of the parrotfish?
Chlorurus gibbus, little macaw-mouthed slick rainbows
crunching on dead coral until their bodies turn it to crystalline granules
of everything we want to escape to, swimming sand factories,
loose cloud explosions as much as 2,000 pounds of sand per year
from each little parrotfish.
What is the heaviness you carry and let go?

I like to look at the numbers of it all—like there are
seven quintillion five hundred quadrillion grains of sand in the world.
How does one even quantity the infinitesimal?
Yet, we do. We have to categorize and number,
define and organize so we can fall into the illusion of mastery
and ownership over all our so-called dominion, but all that sand,
all that incomprehensible universe of whittled-down everything
will outlast all of our counting, speaks of time
in a language we can't even hear.

My dog says   *I love you*
from the other room.

THIRST

for Colocasia esculenta

This morning's wonder
is brought to you by the way
an elephant ear can hold a drop of water

as if in a wide green cup held in its own sentience,

how it sits on the leaf in a perfect globe,
unflinching in its wholeness,
a sphere of light catching an early slant of sun rising.

The drop does not roll away,
does not disappear into the chlorophyll of it all,
just holds steady in the elephant's impermeable insistence.

Who notices these moments but the poets?

Who takes the time to write lines of the way light shines
through a single drop of water poised there on the morning leaf?

Who sings the songs of these unheralded miracles but us minstrels—
scribbling away in our quiet rooms,
mumbling in our lonely corners,
where we pray
in poems
that these miracles never cease
to find us

our eyes
and hearts open

thirsty

for a single drop.

Aerial Caterpillar Ballet

for Halysidota tessellaris

On my daybreak rounds, I spot a tiny acrobat,
swinging wildly in the breeze. White, thorny little wiggler, possible stingers,
a tufted tutu of spikes, dressed in golden morning light,
a pale tiger moth caterpillar almost too small to identify
dancing in the wind like that, her red head glinting in the rising sun.

I wonder to myself, how—
how is this lilliputian creature conducting her own aerial ballet,
and I, her only audience, marveling as she bounces to birdsong,
writhes wildly, flipping and floating, bobbing in the forest before my eyes,
spinning with all of her cares tossed to the treetops,
her ballerina body bending in glorious arcs—
how am I the only one seeing this right now?
Am I imagining this? Am I dreaming? Am I high?

On a typical morning where I could've used a miracle,
watering the garden and thanking the flowers for being flowers,
suddenly she appeared, gleaming like a Tinkerbell rendition
in a community theater children's play of Peter Pan,
rappelling down from the rafters
            or a tall mighty oak   or heaven
on an almost invisible silk line, right to my line of sight,
plump tiny spiky angel in white, whirling like a dervish,
spinning the moment holy, dancing ecstatic in all her freedom—

bungee cord shot from her mouth in a liquid stream,
and as soon as it touched the air
becoming fine silk, spinneret miracle moving through her lips,
dancing from her own daring to drop from the sky.

O, how I wish my words,
spinning silk-pure from the consciousness of my heart,
would tumble out from my lips, touch the willing air,
and become something someone else could hang onto
or a golden thread I can hold onto myself
when I am f r e e f a l l i n g
so I might
dance without fear
in a daring aerial ballet of my own.

ROSE-BREASTED

for Pheucticus ludovicianus

To be rose-breasted
as in the grosbeak that graced
the feeder today on my lunch-break,
me, in my teaching clothes, bright red beret,
black shirt buttoned to my neck covered in roses,
somehow a reflection before this auspicious landing.

I sit on the bed with my shoes on because I have to leave again soon—
my wife has been sneezing and coughing, so I brought her a pharmacy run
of cough drops allergy meds kleenex, and from bed she's been watching
the spring migration landing outside our bedroom window.

I bring both our binoculars to bed and for a moment here we are,
lunch-break lovebirds peering close and hopeful, then there!
A sudden flash of black white and roses—he lands!
A rare vibrant specimen, gorgeous Rose-breasted Grosbeak,
his feathers
        red like summer tomatoes
        red like fire-engine cry
        a red blazing sunrise cutting through the sky

and I've been teaching simile and metaphor all morning
to fourth-graders at the school down the road,
so all I see are figurative languages in the way he perches there—
a rose blooming in mid air,
        the roses on my shirt,
            the roses in my heart rising,
                rose-breasted chest bested only
by this flying mirrored birdsong
quiet flutter   feeding on seeds during my lunch-break

our binoculars glinting in the noonday sun.

RED-WINGED BLACKBIRDS IN ELAINE, ARKANSAS

for Agelaius phoeniceus

All the blackbirds have red wings here.

They dive bomb the fields swaying with cotton blooms.
Red-winged Blackbirds, almost suicidal,
diving into the aerodynamic wind currents of my speeding car,
down solitary country road to desolate town,
an abandoned school turned museum of grief,
mausoleum of ancestral trauma.

Here—September 30th, 1919, a massacre without true headlines.

Here—Unabashed murders of Black sharecroppers,
Black women and children,
gunned down and hunted by the hundreds.

White farmers. White guns. White hate.

Black bodies, no southern trees,
just fields and fields of empty haunting, Black ghosts in bloom.

The children's children stay, say *we are still here—*
this land was picked clean with their grandfathers' hands,
worked and tilled with cotton-pricked fingers,
blood running into the soil,
fertile with their whitewashed forgetting,
the mass grave of their silencing.

All the blackbirds have red wings here.

They sing in fields and fields of cotton
bleeding streaks of color
as they lift up in a chorus of flight

      open wounds
          bright
          against the Black.

This Too

yesterday
i knocked out
all my own lights
hid the key to the switch
under my own split tongue
put my fist through something
immovable so i could hit
myself back
and when i came crawling
back to myself
to apologize
to my reflection
i could only look into
my glimmering sad eyes
and pull that closed up little girl
close into my chest
and say

don't worry
this too
is progress

Just Talk

I was taught to swallow my pain—
not to talk through it
not to talk it out
not to express it but to hold it in
a blade made poison
not to make more waves
than the tsunamis already crashing

ancestral DNA strands leave me stranded
without a lifeline to cling to
when it comes to conflict
to confrontation
to chaos

asian quiet subservience
wanting to break free
from
a history of martyrs
a lineage of resentful sacrifice
heavy laurels of suffering

pain does not bring holiness

mid-life
still
I run
like a mouse
hide like a child
in the repressed emotional state I still trigger slip into
hazardous cliff of psyche and I can so easily veer off track
dangerous unprocessed hole
and I am the rabbit swirling down down down

communication roots in commune
to share one's intimate thoughts and feelings with someone else
especially on a spiritual level
communication
does not have to be scary, little girl

think of the weight lifted through voice
think of the sudden wings

the elephant in the room
is my own bursting wide heart

waiting
        to embrace womanhood
waiting
        to tell the child in me to speak
waiting
        to hold her gently to my chest then release her
waiting
        to sing the music of our perfect cells

I'm clutching onto stars
to find a way out of a biography of dark—

the light has been in my mouth all along

I Screenshot a Woman on Zoom

because while I read my poems aloud   her box is like a painting
her virtual window is some other world I want to peer into
and hold
a new ekphrastic—there   living
still   life

renaissance mouth rose dusted with color
skin porcelain like a moon waxing
and her delicate hand resting behind her long neck
thin forearm draping pale against the black of her sweater
elbow resting on unseen knee
such softness
from another era entirely
such sincerity in her languorous gaze
the orchids and white roses huddled from winter
greening at her shoulder
safe in her space

I want to hold this stare
simply for the unfolding art of her
for the way I am sure she never sees herself
a reflection of anonymous grace

and lest I forget what first caught my eye—
the thick brown-golden braid hanging over her shoulder
half undone   falling free
but the three parts   still   holding on
untied   a suggestion of wildness
horse-like
an untethering
loose long and slowed down

perhaps she was in the middle of undressing the day
and remembered a poetry reading on zoom
a chance to stare softly into windows
peer into other worlds
walk through
a gallery of light

I Sit with a Master

for Jane Hirshfield

I sit with a Master of poetic craft, her essays,
the nine gates of her soul-piercing words
under the blazing sun overhead.

I lie down on the mahogany deck, and it warms my back with ambient fire.
I radiate   and my heart opens like a cracked hymnal as I read.
The book is surrounded in blue sky above and moving
white clouds that swirl in a dance around this learning,
this prayer of attentiveness,
this call to concentration her words bring forward.

I live this way already, tuned to a higher frequency, a foot in both worlds.
I tread the trails of stars while dipped in this humanness.

Attentiveness.   Observation.
                    Attentiveness.   Observation.
                                                            Breath.

All of my eyes are open.

My cells divide into infinities.
I taste this moment with all of my bodies—
the book's slick cover and grainy pages,
the summer morning's soft breeze, the billowing nimbus,
her trusted voice coming through ink,
transcendence
in the ability to stop time
and become a part of every moving cell around me,
the abundance of gratitude that wells inside my body
knowing I can speak the language that pulses in all things,
knowing silence is its own music,
knowing I have been trained to talk unashamed to flowers,
to hear the woodpecker hollow out a song into pine,
to move with the dragonfly ablaze on the corner of the page right now
landing divine on the dog-eared pyramid as if dipped in gold,
the sun kaleidoscoping his wings with another planet's iridescence.

Attentiveness.   Observation.
                    Attentiveness.   Observation.
                                                            Breath.

All of my eyes are open.

I try to catch all the images moving
like salmon swimming in a stream before me,
try to hold them, slippery and fleeting, in an act of poetic preservation,
but there is no stopping the passing of everything as it dances
with everything.

Suddenly a hummingbird
whirrs over me
pauses
in a momentary hover of color
and pees
on my forehead.

Dare I call it nectar of the gods?
Sugar-sweet ambrosia?
A baptism?

Dare I call myself anointed?

Dare I?

Pipe Organs Inside a Japanese Wind-Chime

for Chalybion californicum

My god, it's so hot everywhere.
Seventeen million gallons of sewage
just spilled into the ocean over breakfast.
Redwoods matchstick and mountains weep charred snow.
Another twenty-one wild species become history.
Oceans rise from icecaps melting and calving into the sea,
all while we pretend we're surviving intersecting calamities—

and reader, I just want to go outside,
turn off the world breaking
and listen
as a metallic blue mud dauber wasp
vibrates a song no one has ever heard but me.
I swear it—tenor of hope here
inside the bellowing giant barrels of the precision-tuned
Japanese wind-chimes my mom gave us as a wedding present last year.

And now this maternally-expecting nesting bright blue thing
makes a tunnel of music inside a black metal pipe,
singing a song of resilience in one of the higher chimes,
if I had to guess, in the key of G, yes
here she is—blue blur building cradles of mud,
creating a pipe organ inside her own church,
this gorgeous buzzing and building,
reverberating almost through our whole house
if you listen close enough,
powered in flight
by the nectar of flowers,
and don't you wish
you could say the same thing of yourself?

Honestly, I don't know where this poem is going,
but today the heartbreaks and disasters
both global and deeply personal
are answered in this holy song,
this tenor of building
and buzzing
building
and buzzing

building
and buzzing

a mother's unseen labor,
tuning-fork of the universe
funneled down into mud-making,
a tunnel to some kind of good light,
a nest for something to vibrate through—

be it sorrow,
be it prayer,
be it love,
be it hope of making it
to the other side of all this dark.

Listen.

I said, listen.

Turn off the world breaking
and listen—

a mother is quietly building something out of nothing.

The natural world still finds a way to sing.

FOLD ME INTO PAPER

for my love of sixteen years and counting, Joann

The first wedding anniversary gift is paper,
so, my love, fold me into paper—

take everything I have and fold me into you.
My darling wife, take this wide open life
and crease new lines in me
with the tips of your fingers,
origami my body to yours,
peace crane my hands
to the wings of your heart.

We have been forever joined,
affixed like our silent roots underground,
entwined for lifetimes in this forest of blooming.
We have loved each other since we were trees.
We have arrived here joined in the whirling infinite
through the gifts of each other's longing,
the treasure of each other's searching.

Yes, fold me into paper—
take the selves of my past
made into hemp, linen, wood pulp,
ground me into bamboo juices,
and form me into blank page,
pages of this love story we keep writing,
incarnation after incandescent incarnation.
Remember when we were stars, darling?

Here, take the papyrus of my breastbone
and inscribe your holy name there,
write it in fire, in blood,
in the inky stain
of forever,
to have and to hold,
infinitely, I do,
again and again, I still do
take you
as my wife, as you
take me.

Fold me into paper
and let me keep writing poems
to the life-shaped grace of your heart,
to the way you sword the light in people,
to how you give and give and give,
let me give you all these poems
pages and pages of paper,
flying like birds.

Fold me into paper
press your red lips to this fresh canvas,
mark me with your everlasting kiss,
the bliss of this life infused
into every undivided cell of me.

Fold me into paper,
build us into a little dreamboat
sailing on an ocean of tenderness,
floating on gentle waves
of always making each other laugh,
of always speaking with truth and conviction,
of always searching for light and beauty
and running with that beauty
in our origami hands
to show each other
another wondrous infinite thing,

our love
is a wondrous infinite thing—
since we were trees,
since we were whispering roots reaching,
since we were stars spinning together,
and into whatever our love becomes, darling,

fold me into paper
and fold me, hold me, beside you.

Loving an Old Dog

for Canis lupus familiaris

Sometimes, he sleeps at my feet while I write poems
and his snores are the music my heart slow dances to,
and yes, it's true, that if he is really quiet,
sometimes I will check to see
that his belly is moving up and down,
rising and falling like a soft tide,
check that he is still breathing while he sleeps.

      It's a trick I learned as a kid
            when my mom had a heart attack in her forties.
      I just watched her sometimes as she slept,
          made sure she was still here,

how I want to make sure he is still here,
our only son
who wears a suit of fur—
      his quiet tufts of love and protection,
         his bright smiling smooshed face,
            his never-ending boundless grace.

We used to wrestle every day.
He has a stuffed brown buffalo
puppet that I make come alive with my hand.
Man, he and Buffalo-Fluffalo used to tussle
and push and flop and roll and bounce together,
furry wrestle-mania friend attached to the end of my hand,
and we don't wrestle too much anymore,   no,   not like before,
but that playfulness is still there, that light-filled joy.
His fiery soul roars in his little lion being,
and I know in his spirit, he's still a young pup
with a young heart—it's just that his body
is getting along in years.

And it's okay if he can't make it all the way
around the circle driveway anymore on our evening walk.
We are glad to lift him into our arms,
walk most of the way holding him,
his proud boxcar chest out, sniffer up in the air,
tail a slow wagging, a couple of licks on my cheek.
We will gladly become his legs,

set him down in the soft patches
where he still kicks up the grasses wildly,
leaves his marks on our land
then walks the rest of the way home,
waits to make sure all the girls get into the door first,
because he is quite the gentleman,
the gentlest man I know,
always has been,
the embodiment of tenderness,
if love had four legs.

And he's not going anywhere
anytime soon if we can help it,
he, the yang in our yin-yang Pekingese pair,
the temple Fu dog with a heart of gold.

As I write this poem, through my open office window
a red fox screams in our summer night woods
over and over as if in agreement with these words,
as if to say in wild canine song—

> *Genghis is more than an old dog,*
> *Genghis is what every one of us strives to be.*

I remember when we first moved to Arkansas,
Genghis howled a low song of thanks to three wolves,
but that's another story, another poem,
now—a fox through a window of trees sings back to him, full circle.

Sleeping underfoot,
Genghis hears the night fox, lifts his head,
and I swear I see him smile before he goes back to sleep—
the song of snoring dreams and fox screams
entwining in a language that builds
invisible bridges under stars.

Without Saying It, a Poem about the *

So many times I have looked up at your face with a question,
waited in your silver light   to feel a dance   to feel heard and seen
Is this a dream?   Is this what a mirror looks like as a planet
            as a silent giant   as a friend?

I sat underneath you for hours last night, admired how you paint the leaves
luminescent   without even trying. I tasted your pale mouth—
felt the blue drape of your gaze fall across the pines, your omniscient eyes rise through
the still air, and I'm just happy someone is watching.
            My body the anchor   you the tender elliptic h/lover.

I see how you reflect movements in water of night frogs and fish,
creating ripples of life-light. Your face stirred in waves, your fullness
absorbing   my ache   my helpless   my silence
my empty   my whole.

Dear round sister—   Dear golden howl magnet—
Dear garland of starlight resting on your brow—   Dear woman rock—

Why do you persist in this infinite dance?   This everlasting circle of regret?
What can I understand about the shape of your sadness?
How it comes back and comes back   or is it just reflection?

You are a dead planet yet I am still in awe of your light,
or more accurately the way you bounce it off your body back
into my waiting chest, into this cavern of want I call sternum,
into the oceans inside me rising to meet you.

I take you inside me—gentle sphere, constant variable, habitual shrine.

How many times have I looked up at your face with a question
knowing the answer is buried in my own heart?

It's the way you give that heals me, the way your silver speaks
in quantified fragments of deliverance—your newness, your quartered halved face
your fullness   again   again   always up there   watching me watch you

*moon

My First Mammogram

I make my hospital gown a flowery superhero cape around my neck
and I watch as the cross-sections of my breast
appear on the huge high-definition screen in front of me

the radiologist calls my breast
beautiful
not a medical word, not some cold opaque language
but *beautiful*
the word hangs in the air for a moment
and she is a devoted monk in pink scrubs
bowing at the temple of woman

my breast there   in the light and shadow
the black and whites splayed
like a glowing orb
I didn't even know I held inside until now

and I say *oh wow*   *it looks like a planet*   *or a full moon*
of course I am a poet
and everything can look like a moon
if you open yourself enough to light your reflection
and I tell her I am a poet so naturally
I make these moon references and she laughs

and together with new eyes and no words
we see the lunar tides
in the soft light waves of my breast
see that I contain rotund multitudes
there on the screen
prominent nipple white in its denseness
spinning some new cosmos within my milky ways

I contain vastness unnamed but held in my chest
multitudes moons planets lines cells
here in this body
here in this beautiful body
here in this beautiful celestial body

glowing
before me

III.

BREASTFEEDING WITH TRICERATOPS

The massive bones of a triceratops gleam in the stark darkness
and my sister's heart moves in accordance to her baby boy's hands,
his eyes gleaming at the massive bones and teeth
of dinosaurs shining white in a dark room,
her eyes gleaming bright at the sight of his wonder.

There is so much contrast here—extinction museum,
menagerie of asteroid dust, great hall of skeletal secrets maneuvered
to loom how they would have appeared in the epoch of their grandeur.

White bones and dark collide in his eyes and baby boy gets hungry—
so much to soak in   a filled glass of consciousness.

He shapes his mouth an O
               to drink   to suckle   to nurse   to ground his infant flights.
Light and shadow manifest in mesozoic matriarchy
paleontology   sweet milk   bright bones   profound juxtapositions of extinction
and birth   and I am a witness to this tender history.

My sister was sometimes a shy girl, never wanted too much light cast on her
but as a mother, it is only the glow of her growing son
shine   she follows.

She sits in the middle of the dimly-lit museum, giant dinosaur
bone puzzles standing like prehistoric guards as crowds walk by.
She makes her body a bassinet, wraps her scarf over baby's little head
which he pulls down with baby hands to unblock his brontosaurus view.
Stimulation and comfort enchant him in a warm swaddle.
His eyes dart around at hovering pterodactyls attached by cables from the ceiling.

He nuzzles suckles smiles   face ablaze with curiosity
lips forming a circle that cannot be broken
through layers and layers of eons and ice ages. This is timelessness,
the infinity loop between mother and child, breast to mouth, heart
to growing heart, and I stare in wonder at the miracle of this simple act—
seeing my little sister   break past me for a moment   in evolution
her young clutching everything he needs
to survive.

Xander's Words

I watch as words find themselves in his tiny mouth,
nephew sponge, new life soaking in all life,
to see the wonder, the bright receiving
of all that flickers, floats, shines with color.

He wakes up from a nap and his first word is always *"Light"*
       Light.   *Ball.*   *Key.*   *Tree.*

Butterfly becomes *"by"*
a merging of syllables into one small morsel, *"by"*
and he points his finger to a flying flower that I'd never noticed
in a painting on a wall in a room I know so well.

Dinosaur becomes *"di"*
and he knows it's a dinosaur,
but he doesn't know his mother Diana goes by that same name.
Di, he calls her, again, again, *Di*
as the yellow dinosaur flops in his hand.

The sounding, the repetition, the power of language
becoming synapses firing in a forming consciousness,
the tender music of his mouth repeating and learning words—
I have never felt language like this and language is my life!
Words are my movements through the world, and he is making language
fill with wonder and magic and meaning again   for me.

Kai.   *Kai.*   *Kai.*
He says my name, knows it before we even meet face to face,
learns the face to the name in my FaceTime smile,   *Kai.*
O, praise my mono-syllabic fortune!

I have never heard a more pure vibration than my name on his little lips,
escaping the 16-month-old body of a friend I have known for lifetimes.

Light.   *Ball.*   *Key.*   *Tree.*   *Kai.*

This tiny child, shaping beauty   so much beauty with his mouth,
learning the entire world one word at a time.

Unicorn

The little girl in the post office doesn't know me, but she turns around and says *oh hiiiii* and waves real big and wavy, and shows me her brand new pink shoes that light up a little at the heel, and I say *are those your new shoes? They are so pretty* because you have to talk to toddlers and smile when they talk to you, if you're a decent person, right? And she looks down at them and nods all smiley. I love talking to toddlers, more than adults most days, and I think she's probably almost two, all soft blonde curls and bright baby blue eyes, a literal cherub in broad daylight. Her mother says she's a sponge, just hearing and saying and repeating everything, brand new words and brand new world around her. She shows me her new dress, all of its colors and stripes of rainbow. She says *this is my dress! This is my chooos!* We make (very) small talk as her mom takes care of the packages. She hides under the postal window countertop like it's her own tiny little house, her very own personal cubbyhole, and I so want to crawl under there, too, maybe have a tea party or talk about flowers, but I just watch from my 6-ft socially distanced X-mark, next in line. She picks up a sticker on the floor, maybe a corner of a stamp, and wants to put it on the wall but it doesn't stick, almost puts it in her mouth on her tongue, before I tell her *no no no that's dirty honey* and open the flap of the trash bin to have her throw it away. She bumbles over adorably and throws away the tiny scrap. *Emme*, she keeps saying, *Emme!* I ask, *Is that your name?* Mom answers, *No that's her best friend's name. Her name is Trinity, but she can't say it yet,* and I think of that newness, roll it around on my tongue, the so-new-you-can't-even-say-your-own-name-yet new, that the syllables haven't even found her sounds. Trinity. Trinity. I say her name in my head, as mom and little wingéd thing hold hands and turn to leave. *Bye Trinity!* I say smiling really wide, and she turns and waves all big and wavy, with her whole arm, bright curls bouncing, heels all aglow, *bye-bye!* Her sweetness lingers a few moments in the air after they leave, that pure vibration, and I know I am not the only person in the post office who feels its thick nostalgia. On the way home, it pours down rain out of nowhere, I mean torrential, buckets and buckets, in the middle of the day and the sun is also shining, mind you, so the moment is a mix of bright slants of light pouring through dark clouds, and downpour. I'm following a truck pulling a horse trailer that kicks up the mist from the wet road suddenly drenched, rain easing up now, the sun shining in from the west and golden. The slants of sunlight turn the mist kicking up in the tires into a rainbow, and I am literally following a rainbow all the way home, disappearing and reappearing again with the curves of the road, a path of color in the kicked up mist beaming, and the rain easing and the sun still persistently shining, and perhaps that little girl's rainbow has transcended space and time, her innocent joy lingering as fresh magic, and the sponge of her little bright heart is squeezing out all over my ride home, and maybe that trailer isn't pulling a horse at all, but a unicorn. Yeah, I bet there's a unicorn in there. For sure.

Night Blooming Cereus / Queen of the Night

for Selenicereus grandiflorus

We only ever had an apartment balcony, what my mother turned
into a small flourishing garden of pots spilling over
with what I didn't care to know about as a child.

After her third work shift, I remember her out there at night
bent over against the harsh moth-circled light, tending to quiet green
bodies that reached for her, as she stared out past the rows of cheap housing,
searching inside for her village horizon rice farm mother brothers sisters
back home in the Philippines.

I remember she would wake us up, bleary-eyed children,
and usher us out onto the humid apartment balcony
to show us the night-blooming cereus,
the wild bright opening,
a temporary queen bursting with fragrance,
a silent star stretched out heavy on a long pink neck.
        Look   she would say   *it only blooms once—*
fleeting beauty she served us with the weighted gravity
of losing thick in night's air.

We didn't care much for plants then,
for the display of green she quietly tended
after her third work shift, with her lonely heart.
Children don't care much for the toil, the ache,
the solitude of worry she must've desperately poured
into tender growing things,

changing it all into growth,
transmuting it all into night blooming,
into a balcony of flowering, into waking us up
in the middle of sleep without language to explain a love like this—

how she tended to us,
two tender flowering things,
the toil   the light   the soil

between her tired
beautiful hands.

Damper / She Leaves Paralyzed Spiders in Mud Rooms for Her Unborn Babies

for Chalybion californicum, *again*

Reporting back *(bink)* on the metallic blue
(bink) mud-dauber wasp
making a *(bink)* personal pipe organ
inside our metal Japanese wind-chimes,
(bink) she's building away at a small
nesting *(bink)* complex system of mud
tunnels up through the *(bink)* singing
metal shaft, making holy our music
with her steady *(bink)* growing labor and hum.

It is extra *(bink)* breezy this morning,
the sounds of the six singing wind chimes
(bink) vibrate in the full octave
of their intention as the heavy
wood gongs against them *(bink)*
in the breeze, tubular Japanese harmony
reflecting the *(bink)* zen of the moment,
the music of the spheres,
the *(bink)* melodious movement of
sounds in the air with perfect pitch,
all except *(bink)* one–
all except the muted mud tunnel tube
and its dampered a cappella,
(bink) the softened blow
of that highest-tuned wind chime tube
all chocked and stuffed *(bink)* full of future blues.

She's been busy making separate rooms
for each of her *(bink)* eggs,
at least four mud tunnels *(bink)*
all with their own stacked unknown
chambers, and *(bink)* only in this poem do I
rationalize her motives, her development
song that humans *(bink)* only name as pest,
(bink) her elaborately designed rooms,
her individual *(bink)* living quarters per egg,
her mud-cordoned cells *(bink)*
fortified with spiders she

paralyzes and *(bink)* keeps alive
so her babies can feast on them
(bink) when they wake,

this single mother—
(bink) and all her building,
all her determined working,
all her *(bink)* pupal planning
putting a damper on the music,
muffling *(bink)* the wind chimes' complete song,
filling our pipes with dreams. *(bink)*

And I'm out here every morning
watering the garden *(bink)* with her persistent
soundtrack of hope singing in the
(bink) breezy background.

Her solitary buzzing and vibrating
inside that tube *(bink)* is something
resonant in the ethers,
(bink) the gentle damper
is a song that says a human
lent her *(bink)* this decadent instrument
to tunnel her children's becoming,
and when I *(bink)* hear that
seemingly discordant
bink,
I think of her
and it makes me smile,
because this song *(bink)*— I know by heart.

I've Been Feeding a Monster

for Acharia stimulea

I've been feeding a monster—
saw the chomps taken from my fiddle-leaf fig
and when I bent at the waist, as I do, for a closer inspection, there he was,
small horned verdant horse, saddleback caterpillar with his lime green saddle
and brown spikes slowly slugging his way across the leaf's veiny interior,
and reader, how could I not love him?

In the larval stage, this becoming-moth, apparently,
is one of the most venomous caterpillars in the region,
and I must've felt his aura of sting, his slow mosey of danger,
when normally I would pretend my finger into twig
and welcome a crawling thing onto my palm,
but his spikes screamed *no!*   his alien face screamed *no!*
his stark markings screamed *no!*   his thorny tentacles screamed *no!*
his bright saddle screamed *do not ride!*
horns on both sides, and I could not hide my curiosity.

        I named him my little monster, endearingly.

The spines on the saddleback caterpillar are fragile
and will break off into a predator's body, even become airborne,
embedding into surfaces, flying through the breeze like tiny poison darts,
and within a few minutes, this little monster stole my heart.

I brought a large-mouthed mason jar outside, stuffed two fat green ficus leaves
into the glass and taxied the little beast on the side of a leaf into his new temporary home.
It's for science I told my wife. I wanted to observe his quiet life, see him in stages, rejoice
his instars—how even monsters can transform.

After a day, I felt sad with him sitting alone in the jar, so I put him back
on the ficus and gave him free rein to live in my houseplant outdoor summer forest
as long as he wanted, searching daily for new chomps taken
out of ficus flesh, half circles bitten through to light.

I tendered his thorny tentacled protuberances, smiled when I found him some days
on the underside of leaves, discovered discarded exoskeletons of growth,
until one day there was no spiky darling monster staring back at me.

He's probably a moth now, doesn't even think about me, actually never did.
Saddle gone, unbridled from his instars—wild little horse flying free.

ODE TO RAMEN NOODLES

I know you are no good for me, boxed little square of noodles,
pennies per package, fried plastic encased curly   never-ending
your sodium packet speaks of doom.
I swim with you in your 3-minute heaven.

When I was a kid, mom was always working. Single with two girls
and a new country   early mornings   late nights,
ramen noodles, you were a meal we could manage
ourselves, latchkey kids home from school alone.
Boil water, drop in the noodles, stir in the seasoning, instant dinner, warmth.
We even called you mama, not ramen,
though we knew your name, sounded close enough,
no substitute of course but still there to nourish with outstretched arms,
there to act as pseudo-support system,
as succulent satisfaction   as sacrament   as surrogate.

I know you are no good for me.
As a woman I know your hidden dangers—
your too many grams of carbs, your ungodly amounts of sodium,
your shelf life of forever, but what about the benefits
of comfort foods calling up soul? What about reaching into the past
and finding safety in a bowl of entangled love? Doesn't that mean more?
Your calories won't keep me away for too long. You are the indulgence I dive into
maybe once a month, the fiery taste of childhood's home.

Mom taught us to roll up little meatballs
or cut up a food-stamp hotdog with a butter knife,
toss it into your bubbling water with crunchy bok choy, wilting cilantro,
sprinkled bean sprouts, half a plump lime squeezed, a hard boiled egg,
tiny pickled Thai chili peppers, sriracha until you swirl in a deep dance of red.
I have learned to dress up my nostalgia—
so painfully spicy I can barely eat you but I do. You know I do.
I sweat, nose runs, tears of remembering swirl into your stock
my mouth waters even now as I write because you are always there
bowl of ropes I can cling to when the world spins out of control
ramen noodles gathered in chopsticks, steam rising to meet my mouth
swallowed inferno of asian spice, a hearth I build by myself
and cozy up to alone, golden thread of barely enough to sustain me,
pennies per package   but priceless.

O, ramen noodles—what have you tied back together inside me?

GENDER IS FLUID

My wife and I met a couple of tweens yesterday,
grandchildren of a friend, a sister and younger brother bored at a party,
the kind of outsider kids who magnetized to me when I taught high school.
We struck up a conversation—we'd rather talk to the young ones anyway,
hear their ideas, reflect back their light, share some hope.
They opened like blooms, sensitive, beautiful.

This morning while putting on makeup side by side
in the double mirrors of our bathroom, my wife said—

You know something? When I see a person, I don't really see a he or she,
I see a Soul, but I thought the whole time he was a she wanting to be a boy
so I used HE and HIM when talking to him, but his sister said "this is my brother"
and he really IS a he. He really was her brother. Did I use the wrong pronouns?

And I remember the young binary-bending boy from yesterday,
hair draped like black curtains on either side of their face, their softness,
black nail polish painted on long fingernails, black eyeliner and
mascaraed eyelashes framing crystal blue eyes that I swear saw
into our souls as though from some distant alien galaxy,
with that kind of knowing, and I said—

Don't worry, honey. They could feel your heart.

The young ones today are like water, they don't fit into our squares.
The box of binary is only a limitation for their expansive expression,
and we—the generations before this Z and Alpha,
we try to fit them into our black and our white,
we try to color them inside the lines,
we cram them into confines
because that is where WE came from,
when they—(they/them)—
they are like water, clear-eyed in their autonomy,
they are like sun burning through -isms making rainbows,
they are like diamonds prismatic in their non-conforming facets,
and I remember the boy, the they-them-he-she-all-into-one and no labels
at the same time, and those eyes, those big bright beautiful blue eyes
lined in thick dark eyeliner
as if to say *look*—

look here   look in this mirror at what you could be
if you believed   you, too,   are limitless.

SKYWRITING

for Sky Ezra Grey

I write *skywriting* in my calendar for our writing date we've set together, to meet in the coffeeshop to remember we are *indeed* poets, despite the world breaking at every line, and penciling in the reminder for *writing with Sky* turns into *skywriting* and suddenly I am cloud bound and blue, a chubby little airplane chugging up along the horizon to the open sky, looping cursive poems into the stratosphere.

Pilots have been writing in the sky since 1913 or thereabouts, and over a hundred years later, here I am. I mean, here we are—sitting in a coffeeshop that stirs heavy-metal playlists into their cappuccinos in the middle of the day, and we are two quiet pilots with pens, scratching against the rhythms and drums and sounds of other conversations. And honestly—I can't write like this, in the hum and rush of others. I hear everything too closely, feel the energies left in the room that imbue the hue of who I am when I name myself poet. Truly, I am just here to sit beside you, to write while you write, even if what I write is about why I can't write, just so I am writing with you, and you feel right in a world that tries to tell you every day that who you are **is wrong.**

I am here not writing on the page but holding my heart up next to your pen just so you know you are held, that the page of your life will never be blank because I wait in the margins to catch you if you fall, the lines of worry that write across your top-surgery-scarred chest spell out a story that I know by heart, and even when we sat down to start writing, I knew the poem I was going to write was just sitting beside you—no words, just being.

Just writing beside sky. Just skywriting a poem that lifts his heart a little more to the clouds, to the sun, to some higher horizon than here where people fear what they do not understand, but brother, take my hand.

This poem waits to take shape when I sit again with the phrase *Skywriting*—

I am home now and you are home, and its been days since our writing date, weeks maybe, but I know the words will come because I trust them to, trust that the little chugging airplane of my heart will lift and these small engine combustions will paint my cursive puffy white cloud poem across the blank sky of a page where you can look up out your window from the ground below and know

I love you.

I TALK TO FLOWERS

I don't know about you
but something within me has changed,
some threshold has been crossed, and I am answering
buds and petals calling to me   unfurling
in all their intimate tender splendor—

I talk to flowers, reader, it's true,
call them each by name,
gardenia, with her velvet white kisses,
knockout rose reaching up with her perfect pink poses,
hibiscus, *oh hi, biscus, hey, how are you feeling?*
coneflower and chrysanthemum,
zinnia and hydrangea, lantana and cleome,
bromeliad, a million bells—
I mean they are practically friends,
their music of names,
their beaming colors,
their opening hearts of light,
the way they call to me inside the house,
whisper in their spectrums of decadence for me to come
outside to water them, come be their rain,
a seduction almost that I am afraid to put into words.

Night blooming jasmine, O lady of the night—
when the windstorm tore off one of your
vining branches about to flower wildly,
I wept at the lost possibility of all your aching fragrance,
the almost of your blooms swirling into our bedroom window,
breaking some barrier to past lifetimes in Persia,
now broken and wilted there on the deck,
limp in the lonely after-storm morning.
I mourned you for days,
          darling, I'm sorry.

Yes, I talk to flowers
and even though they don't talk back
in words,
I hear them
louder than everything being destroyed.

SUPERBLOOMS

the wildflower superblooms in the California desert
can be seen from outer space—
why
is there space
between our bodies
when these bodies of color
are reflecting the light of stars?
are mirroring some kind of daylight heaven?
distant galaxies of poppies bloom underfoot
from satellites, colors paint the planet
splay their rich warmth on the curvature
of desert hillsides and valleys

so vast the expanse—
breaths taken away by awe
delicate poppies opening their millions of petals
every day as the sun arches the sky
every night curling up closed
bending their millions of heads in supplication
asking forgiveness
for humanity
for they know what we have done
and what we continue to do

wildflowers need not ask for prayer
when they themselves
are
prayers
answered
of droughts
unholy dry desert lips cracking open
to reveal fields and fields of
boundless hues
and all of their soft colors
darling
only make me think of   you

Requiem for a Small Wild Thing

the terror scream
of death
shoots
in a tone
that is familiar
even if you've never heard the sound
can be recognized without ever being seen

summer hot night
the open bedroom window
the dark darkness
4am
a small animal
        fast squirrel
                possible rabbit
                        is caught by hungry fox

lets out his final scuttle-cry-shriek
waking us to a sound
we knew
but had never heard—

his body
swallowed   night   hush

spirit
        already flying

GOLDEN WINDOW

I woke up crying
without knowing why
until I turned on the news.

Thousands of sleeping
people in Turkey and Syria
did not wake up from the night before,
were caught in their dreams with instantaneous death
as a magnitude 7.8 earthquake shook them from their lives,
churned their cities with a mouth of destruction,
swallowed whole their homes,
hundreds of buildings reduced to rubble
and bodies trapped in the layers of fallen walls,
thousands buried bloody in a second of world collapse.

There is a three-day golden window
where any likely survivors can still be found.

And here the sun is out
after days-long winter grey.
My wife has piled the dried birdhouse gourds
we grew in the garden last summer
onto the wooden table outside.
They stand like a golden moldy army
with their swirls of beautiful black decaying worlds
patterning their thin skin and fat curves.
When you leave these squash out in the elements
of autumn and winter, they hollow and dry from the inside,
maracas of seeds making music with every shake,
nature's effortless percussion.

She pushes gently with sandpaper in circles
to smooth the rough squash facade,
cuts the exact dimensions of a circle door
and empties teddybear shaped seeds into a waiting bowl,
gutting the dry odd-shaped vining fruit
for future bluebird family home.

She scouts the perfect pine and twines
the Bird BNB facing east.

Facing east my eyes turn toward Gaziantep, Turkey,
a young father pulls his dead infant son
from under concrete and rebar,
his bright red swaddling blanket covered
in white ash and dust from the crumble of civilization,
tiny body limp and silent in his father's arms,
life and death collapse into each other,
and I can still hear him wailing,
his chest breaking into fault lines.

In already war-torn Syria,
a little girl shelters her baby brother with her arm
as ten floors sit on her back, they are both alive, rescued.

A newborn baby is pulled from the wreckage,
still tied by umbilical cord to her dead mother
swallowed by the earth's angry core.

The golden window closes,
41,000 dead and rising
with the dust
of fallen cities.

My heart epicenters.

I sob into the morning,
pull the collective grief into and out of my chest,
an aftershock for the mother yet to see her dead children,
an aftershock for the fallen father, brother, uncle, son,
an aftershock for the young bride's broken vow,
an aftershock for the newborn baby girl surviving somehow,
an aftershock for the war regimes that bombed these lives with before-shocks
before-shocks
before-shocks
before-shocks

I sob into the morning
under the weight of earth's sudden and constant fracturing.

And here the sun
seems almost unfair,
the tenderness of this
simple life that we share,

my wife sanding soft circles into squash,
preparing the next home for a nest of fledglings,
the golden dust rising and collecting on her gentle hands.

HOLLOWING

Truthfully, I haven't had much to do with death,
have not slow dance slipped into and out of his/her hands
but I don't know what I will do
with their beloved bones when I do,
when I do lose them—
my family here, now,   in the future there, then.

How will I dance with the loss of these three everythings of mine—
our foursome of softness that will diminish over time,
this triangle of two furry beings and my wife,
when they all inevitably slip
from me
into a future
that is without them?

Can I make an instrument of this loss? A death rattle dirge?
        Will my lonely bones be the hollowed singing in the trees?

I can only think of wind chimes insofar
that every wind will ring of their memories,
every breeze will breathe their names,
and this is all too painful
to imagine,
to move as a solo corner of a once-loved square,
all my angles turned to angels
and I, here,
rattling in the emptiness
they will leave
behind.

I will not yet make an instrument of this loss,
my bones do not want to learn
how to sing
this imminent lament

hollowing   hollowing   hollowing
each day into the music of ash.

Haunt Me Close

How will I know you are still with me

   after you go from this world too early

for my future to lose you? What will you feel like in spirit form, ghost of love

   not close enough to touch, but just   to know?

How will I know you are watching and listening and pushing up star-ward

   as you do, have always done, my love? Is it so I can somehow

stand on a the ridge-line of a nebula and still taste your kiss, still know

   that everything around me is now

you? Miraculous woman, is that what I shall search for in the mundane? Miracles

   and moments that calculate themselves by the standard of two,

that divide themselves only by the infinities multiplied between us?

   Did I recognize you

already as the heavens, when you were earthbound, enough?

Last night we made love, bent time in shadows cast on walls by candle flame,
and everything is beautiful with you beside me, and to think of life without you—

   a generation between us, but lifetimes shared,

no, no this despair is too much,
let me ask it plain—will you haunt me close, darling,

   when you go, will you haunt me

        please?

IV.

As You Stand in a Field of Diamonds, I Follow You in a Poem

You are hunting for diamonds right now in the rain,
trudging through muck and mud in the after storm,

rain boots and neon coat, like a walking sun
coercing the clouds to part before you, and before you

there were hardly moments that became poems before me,
so how could I not follow you in words today, see you

reaching for shine underfoot, and in my mind, I go there to the field,
wallow in your footprints like a waiting prince of poems

eager to make holy your path with words, ready to scribe the verses
that unfold in your unearthing, your digging always deeper,

your sifting the dirt from the gleaming, light blooming at your feet.
And maybe this is how you found me, hopeless coal waiting

to be a thing that shines, a thing that is reminded of sparks of light
and you are that willing mud walker, coal breaker, woman in the rain,

waiting for the familiar refrain of diamond dust echoing,
a star singing, an unnamed element waiting to be called infinite—

my body cracks into diamond spinal sword and you pull me
out of stone. I see your knees mud-heavy, your rain boots tracking hope,

how beauty is the language that magnets us, how beauty is always
how the poems unfold—me in your path toward finding diamonds,

writing of rainwater falling down your cheek, writing of sudden sun
breaking through clouds, and you there with your flawless heart

calling out to your reflection.

LESBIAN FLOWER

for Sappho

Our hillside is blooming pale purple and blue this morning,
lush with a rush of color after the rains, soft heart-shaped
leaves, pushing up through soil and splaying themselves open
across the meadow, vulnerable, fresh, saying *I am love itself.*

Newly sprung springtime is unfolding and I bend at the waist
into the lushness, don't waste a moment fretting about guessing
the names of these wild flowering things—the naturalist in me
needs their true botanical handles. I zoom in with my plant ID app
and snap to reveal the common blue violet, *Viola sororia*, also known as
lesbian flower—what perfection, what queer botany, what synchronistic bliss
that this wildflower kissing by the thousands the whole of our hillside is called
the lesbian flower, violet, purplish blue sky dropped down to the earth spreading
here at home with supple hearts underfoot. *The violet's nectar* says the app
*is jarred loose by butterflies and bees who must burrow deep inside
the flower to reach its sweetness* . . . lesbian flower, burrow deep, shake
me loose, nectar-sweet blooms all along our wild valley, our hills and curves.

From the isle of Lesbos, Sappho speaks in her Ode to Aphrodite—
      Many crowns of violets, roses and crocuses . . .
      many scented wreaths made from blossoms around your soft throat . . .
      with pure, sweet oil . . . *you anointed me, and on a soft, gentle bed* . . .
      you quenched your desire . . . *no holy site* . . . *we left uncovered, no grove* . . .

This trove of lesbian love language, 10,000 lines of lyrics, burned by men
who could never love with such softness. Only 650 fragments remain
yet here on our hillside, my lover and I walk barefoot in the after-wet rain,
crush violets, their edible petals and heart-shaped leaves, stepping toward
each other's heart-shaped hearts and heart-shaped hands, lips and tongues,
burrow deep for the nectar, edible flowers, lesbian flower, common blue violet,
fragments burned into seeds over millennia blooming here, purpling blue
free and wild, 10,000 lines of lyrics open and blushing lush wet petals, garlands and
wreaths of violets, laurels of violets, laureate of lesbian flowers—I sing
my un-fragmented un-singed song to the poet who gave us her language
of softness   throat neck lips hips thighs
strummed on her lyre the music that pulses pulses pulses perennial
through time and blooms blue here this morning,
my lover and I wet
with rain.

TALKING DIRTY

If I am the dirt,
then plant something
inside me,
root and burrow,
push and push and push,
dig deep within me with your fingers
and drop a flowering seed,
another,
another,
again,
harder,
shovel me closer to you,
make a mound of me beside you,
bury your mouth into my bright darkness,
I will nourish you, I swear,
I will retain your softness, will give and bend,
will pack myself solid to foundation your footing
onto me, take me
in your hands,
let me stain you dirty,
mud your skin
with the earth of me,
if I am the dirt,
then let's never be clean.

Ode to the Hornworm

for Manduca sexta

O, vibrant sticky-footed goblin,
alien lord of some deeper knowing,
great green decimator of tomatoes—
I come to the garden with a plan this morning,
steely-eyed and ready to follow the skeletal remains
of once-blooming foliage and ripening red planets,
ready to come and pick you off   gently
with the gloved fingers of this gardener I've become,
determined to put an end to your destructive hunger,
only to find you there in all of your bright emerald wonder,
your glowing body there on the vine, divine,
invisibly perfect in your chlorophyll camouflage,
bulbous and plump from engorging green, you fattened gorgeous thing.

O, glorious hornworm—
munching *Manduca sexta*,
I cannot pluck you from this desperate plant
without first acknowledging the glory of your stiff red horn tail,
          you backwards-facing predator trickster unicorn,
your white stripes that parallel the lines of leaves,
the shape of your green curvature and swell.
You will devour and deflower an entire
canopy of tomato leaves overnight,
you will scar fruiting dreams, break their tender skins,
shit tiny green grenades with tenacity, grow and grow and grow.

I pluck you, as the tomatoes weep, and lay you in my glove.
Here—let me carry you, just let me look at you
and your insatiable brothers squirming here in my palm,
squishy bodies plump with the pulsing green of life.
You latch your little succulent feet to the vines of my fingers,
and turn yourself sphinx, posture yourself ancient mystery,
lift your torso and head to see with all of your eyes
this human disturbance to your photosynthetic meal,
to you becoming sunlight itself.
Your suctioned feet grip tight to me like velcro
as though mother nature hugs me through your ten back prolegs.

O, (not so) little hornworm of ample proportions,
you dance wild and sectional toward sky
inching toward the unknown, becoming sphinx.

Dear bright one—
how do you get away with such unabashed otherworldliness?
how do you actually become a whole other being?
how do you molt away instars, *in stars?*
how do you teach your bodies
to fall away
when they no longer fit your growth?

Teach me this language of transformation,
teach me I can burrow into darkness
and still come out as hummingbird
moth flower-drinker winged-egyptian almost-bird.

You here,
your verdant brothers,
all brilliant and brimming with the juices of earth
in my hand—
I bow all my fingers toward you,
my you-sized human reflections of thanks,
sphinx my knuckles in gratitude
and move you

far

far away

from my tomatoes.

Making Something That Lasts

Today we're pickling the cucumbers that have been
growing wild and sprawling all through our stone garden,
climbing the other fruiting flowering things
with their unruly tendrils,
swirls of persistent vibrance
spiraling up the giant zinnias,
marrying the yellow squash with their reaching,

just as this poem has   s p r a w l e d
into wild unruly descriptions of the cucumber patch
when I mean to be pickling in the kitchen
with my wife in her matching overalls
singing along to a song playing over the speakers
literally called *The Pickle Song*.

You do silly things when you're married
like wear matching overalls
and dance around the kitchen island
while shoving spears of cucumber into waiting mason jars,

you kiss each other—both holding knives—
and have never felt safer.

She puts a yellow dill flower behind your ear
and you see yellow fireworks
in her blue eyes.

You do silly things when you're married—
there is a level of corniness that sort of laps around on itself,
making it all of a sudden cool,
making it all of a sudden perfect,
making this moment
everything you've actually
ever wished for
hoping

when the mason jars seal tight with a pop,
this feeling will keep forever.

Beyond Us

I don't want all of your tiny secrets,
little almost-invisibles.

The pulsing world vibrates with all this human destruction
and there you are in your small wonder, aching to shape yourself into the vastness,
molecules and mitochondria multiplying into vibrant colonies of life,
mycelia speaking in mush-rooms in a language we cannot hear,
and just recently, a thousand baby praying mantises hatched
in my blooming red anthurium, small murderers wandering
in green blurs, so tiny hiding under leaves in clandestine clusters,
and the friendly jumping spider smiling in the greenhouse corner,
and the green lynx spider with her silk-spun egg sac of hundreds of babies,
and the thick galleries of fiery ants tunneling underfoot,
and the bumblebees bumbling drunk into flower-middles,
and the black frog egg globes gelatinously interconnected
brimming in our small plastic swimming pool,
and the hummingbirds in all of their blurred humming,
vibrating the infinity of the universe in their wings,
and all of the magical and mysterious beings who remain unseen—

I don't want all of your tiny secrets,
little almost-invisibles.

I want you to be safe and free.
I want to offer you shelter in my large largeness,
a human mother animal who just leaves you to be,
there, singing in your unheard frequencies,
living your minuscule miraculous lives that have nothing to do with me—
your breeding and breathing,
your building and feeding, flying and fucking—
your existential beauty is yours,
whether we humans name it or not,
your vastness is more grand in its design than anything our
feeble human minds can even mouth with our heavy tongues.

Keep your secrets, almost invisible ones.

Live and flourish
                              beyond us.

Midwifing Tadpoles in the Anthropocene

for Hyla chrysoscelis

My wife made a siphon with a long black tube,
and through some slow water sorcery, sort of vacuumed up
the hundred or so wriggling tadpoles that were clinging
to the side walls of our small plastic pool,
not to be sucked out into oblivion, mind you, but moved swiftly,
as if worm-holed, into their own private pond we made out of the blue
tupperware bin that used to hold our Christmas decorations,
now a makeshift manger for a hundred or so baby froglets
almosting into their other selves.

And you should have seen their little black bodies
shooting out of that tube all slow motion,
like the softest bullets moving peace,
wiggling into this smaller ocean
one after another until every tadpole
was safely transported into this new den
of development, and normally we would just walk
the big blue container over to the koi pond
and dump them in there to live out their metamorphosis
but the koi fish have been insatiably hungry lately
and that just seemed like a raw deal—
they wouldn't have stood a chance, you know?

So here we are, in the peak of summer,
midwifing tadpoles in the anthropocene,
the epoch of humans changing the climate,
and us in our forest home doubling as wildlife sanctuary
creating a safe little stillness for these hundred or so babies to grow.
What's a few days? we say to ourselves,
then we find out a few days is actually 12-14 weeks
for these squiggly adorable things to become frogs
who can actually fend for themselves and survive.

Maybe mama tree-frog singing her nighttime trills
from the gardenia outside our kitchen window
knew the koi pond was a no-go,
and desperate times called for desperate measures,
so she released her jelly clutches of eggs
into our human hands,
and yes, these are desperate times   everywhere,

and it's about time humans did something for
a species other than our own.

So here we are—
delivering tenderness to tadpoles
for an anonymous amphibian mom.

Is there ever a threshold of tenderness?
I never want to cross it.

Sometimes I go out and sit by the baby blue
transformation station, watch them all wiggle,
give them silly names like Jane and Barnaby,
even brought a couple of floating lily pads
from the koi pond and plopped them in,
tilted a nice stone to the wall, moss,
really spruced up the place,
and they seem to like it,
so here we are—

change protectors,
doulas of evolution,
midwives of metamorphosis,
helping a fellow mother of the world,
who sings her trills of thanks outside our kitchen window
perched on the gardenia branch overlooking
hundreds of her wriggling children.

ONLY THE INFINITESIMAL

for Asclepias tuberosa

It seems I can't get my head out of the magnified graces
of infinitesimal beings swirling all around me in this season of burning,
this stage of heatwaves, wildfires, and cataclysmic human destructions,
this apotheosis of scientific climate warnings
and global temperatures steadily warming,
polar icecaps and glaciers melting into memory,
into oceans' unstoppable rise rise rise flood flood flood.

New York City had a year's worth of rain in a matter of hours,
and I can't get my face out of the flowers,
can't stop watching the honeybee
bouncing from the bright petals of giant zinnias,
coral, violet, red, pink, back to coral—
the perfect electrostatic velcro of her body
pollinating all the colors, playing bee footsie
with small yellow star stigmas open and waiting.

On her hind legs, golden saddlebags
are stuffed swollen with nectar-sticky pollen.
A honeybee can hold a million grains of pollen
in each of those saddlebags, miraculous,
and she is just here, in our garden,
doing her undaunted bidding with the planet—
here with her other honey and bumble friends,
spreading gametes to ovules, propagating flower sex
and sowing hope for some semblance of tomorrow.
She works, dances, dives face-first into colors,
as do the tiny tongues of hummingbirds,
the minute feet of beetles and iridescent wings of butterflies,
all pollinating, so that later   there may still be   life.

I watched a milkweed pod crack open in the summer heat
and reveal dozens of sleeping seeds inside
all lined up like tight soldiers
about to jump from an airplane—
the war   against humans perhaps,
the battle   time,
so glorious is their perfect milkweed seed design.
As they loosened in the wind, I saw each brown seed
was equipped with its own ethereal feathery white parachute,
ready to rise into a drift of air and land in some willing soil

to bury and grow and sprout and feed again
some Monarch,
some unappreciated royalty, perhaps a queen.

These wondrous things are happening
while the world is burning, friends,
and maybe if I name them,
if I lend them my pointed attention
and signal in keys my undivided gratitude,
that vibration will pound its own subtle harmonies
into all of the breaking around us.

If we are, in fact, all connected as matter evolving
to Spirit, perhaps if I genuflect
my poems
to the holiness
of only the infinitesimal,
something will bloom   that is infinite.

Perhaps if I focus
the whole of my cosmic heart
on these minuscule mundane miracles,
I am helping somehow to build a new world,
heavy with my stuffed golden saddlebags
and ethereal feathery parachute,
pollinating the thoughts
that energy can
follow
into manifestation.

Intimacy

Late last night, I ran to you
after writing–you were
glistening and soapy
in a bubble bath, and
I read you
my latest poem
from the edge of the tub
about how honeybees
carry golden saddlebags
of pollen on their hind legs,
dipping face first into flowers,
brushing off the dust of sex into
these nectar-mixed purses
heavy with hope,

and you delighted in
each tender line, splashing
in the same wonder I
had in writing the poem,
your smile glinting
like a pearl underwater,

and I've never made love like this.

Earnestly, I Ask

Wait, don't go.
I don't care that there are 27,
sometimes 28, years between us, my love—
our time together has been timeless,
our sixteen years loving
need at least sixteen more, please,
don't go.

Please wait somehow
for me to age beside your aging,
for my hair to whiten
and grey against the day beside your grey,
for my face to welcome lines of time
the way your beautiful face has
sketched the hours
upon the corners of your eyes,
your cheeks and mouth,
your forehead, darling, wait for me—

I am still a fledgling elder
in your shadow
of wisdom
and flight,
a horizon lies on your hipbones
and my head is in your lap
asking,
        no begging,
please
        wait—
                don't go.

Hoarding the Tangible

One could say I am a hoarder of trinketry, a collector of the concrete,
a magpie of the mundane, as I have a treasure trove
of things tucked away, saved objects that define an experience,
and with a lifetime of memories that faded from my consciousness
at such a young age, crossing an ocean on a plane from Bangkok
and looking back at what was already disappearing,
one could say, out of necessity, that I am a thief   of tiny tangibles.

The concierge didn't notice the small bright red Christmas ball
swiped off the branch of a lit tree in front of the Hotel des Marronniers in Paris,
from the below-freezing holiday with mom as we wandered
the cobbled streets on New Year's Eve, Eiffel Tower champagne-kissed and
frozen iPhones, the GPS of our hearts leading us home finally to the warmth
of our hotel windows glowing with beauty. I bring the red globe back
across the pond with me, like a heart still beating that memory.

I still have the long blue tie from the silk robe
that my wife wore when we first fell in love,
all the times I pulled her into me
by the silky string, how our nights would sing,
and one day she will be a memory
and maybe through this blue worn silk rope
I will still be able to reach her, if I don't ever let go.

I don't let go of things,
keep keepsakes for the sake of keeping myself,
rogue souvenirs from moments that mean something to me,
champagne corks and bottle caps,
pamphlets and torn pages of notebooks,
a reservoir of rocks and smooth stones I always intended to label,
grand canyon, niagara, buffalo river, yosemite, some wild pink desert,
now just a mountain of unknown where-I've-beens
making a new geography in my office.

I have small boxes filled with acorn hats and feathers, colorful dead insects,
flower-crowns dried, and a whole bright yellow wing of a goldfinch,
keepsakes and odd shaped artifacts that only translate
to my own intimate archaeology   and I can unearth
these treasures when I find myself lost in the losing.

Maybe if I hold on to this emotional ephemera,
to this mausoleum of tangibles,

if I lead this small army of knick-knackery into my lonely future,
I can keep the current of these moments close,
I can transmute their psychic frequency into actuality,
I can perform some kind of transient alchemy,
I can remember tomorrow all these blesséd todays.

If I pick up a stone, or a folded origami crane,
or a saved napkin from a Madrid cafe,
or a dried white rose from my wedding day
and I move it
            back and forth and
                        back and forth in my hands,
the moments and places take shape again,
some sort of otherworldly chemistry in the objects
imbued with molecular recollection
of mother, father, sister, friends,
and you, my darling–   (I can see you shaking your head).

        Detachment, you always taught   detachment.
        I know this is a desperate measure, this un-letting go,
        and I won't even divulge my motives to you
        because you are still wide-eyed and here.
        I acknowledge my futile holding on even if it's only in this poem.

And yet, I am a crow for shiny crumbs of this present joy,
a guilty squirrel of mementos.

I will whittle down my museum of (in)valuable treasures,
and unhinge this lock on the door of my mind.
These cold instruments of my fear of losing everything
will never take me back to the now of now,
where you are warm,
where you are still right here–
and when you let go of that blue silk rope,
the world will still be here to get lost in
and to find myself in again,
without a compass
or a folded up napkin
or a champagne cork,
the petals of our dried flowers will scatter in the wind
and become the new earth,

the uncharted geography of tomorrow.

BLACK SNAKE

for Pantherophis obsoletus

Driving home from the vet, where our old dog
gets a ketamine injection for his chronic osteoarthritis pain,
he and I drive by a large black rat snake
splayed bloody and writhing in the middle of our street,
halfway out of his misery   run over
his snake body   glistening   like an oil slick,
his entrails trailing   a   bright   red   pool
organs green and fleshy   protruding   ghastly.

I slow to check on the poor creature,
roll the window down to see if he is dead or not—
thick life stopped short and he moves,
shapes and coils his body
into (I swear) a heart,
a swirl, a sign he's still here yet unsalvageable.
He lifts his head toward me,
his round eyes meet mine
and I think of those cowboy movies
where the gentle sheriff has to shoot his horse
because it's broken its leg clomping through a rocky ditch,
and do I carry this stark compassion in my bones?

          At the moment, no.

I drive home, carry my old dog inside
and tell my wife of the black snake in the road.
Is it suffering? Oh Kai, it's suffering—
she runs out the door, frantically paces the deck for a moment.

          How are you going to do it? I ask.

Don't ask me that question right now!
Tires skid reverse and I walk inside thinking
of pleading snake eyes and a type of bravery that's unnamed—

I look at Genghis, our old sleeping good boy,
his eyes drowsy from the ketamine
but the warmth and love in them still shine
with the trust of a young puppy,
his body   curled   into a heart.

CRASHING TOWARD LIGHT

for Phileurus truncatus

here I write
in the summer of fire in the year of drought
in the age of unreasoning   in a biosphere of bombing
in the epoch of endless suffering—

what of this world is left for poems?

surely not this giant triceratops beetle
ambling in the dark across my kitchen floor,
his horns glinting some far off light as I flip on the switch

not his slow steady walking
            toward some unseen extinction
                    some critical mass
not the glass I reach for   the stiff white paper
how I dome over and slide him into momentary captivity
coo at his jurassic beauty
photograph him as he shines his glorious blackness

does it become a poem
when I see a spiderweb's stringy silk
tangled on his barbed leg and across his face?

does it become a poem
when I swirl the cotton candy webs off him with a toothpick
clean him like he is mine before releasing him back into the wild night?

lately I have been bathing small creatures
like some residue of being a childless mother—
a muddy baby green anole lizard the other morning
with the mist of garden hose as he curled in my hand
now this prehistoric present sweet beetle stealing my heart

google says the triceratops beetle also called the loving scarab *crashes toward light*
flies with a force toward all that is bright and warm

what a way to live   or die

crashing toward light

Things I Love about This Generation of Queer Kids

I love their courage.
I love their refusal of closets.
I love their chosen names.
I love their use of the singular *they* pronoun.
I love their blurring of binaries.
I love their honesty.
I love that they go to therapy
        and work to heal themselves like we never did.
I love their healing,
        how it somehow heals backwards through generations.
I love that they set boundaries and choose families.
I love their hairstyles and hair color, how they change like mood rings.
I love the pride they wear on their backpacks,
        their scrunchies, their clothes, their pins, their eyelids.
I love their fierce goodwill thrift-store outfits.
I love that they are not afraid to love each other.
I love their tenderness and vulnerability.
I love their empathy, how deeply they feel.

I love their freedom—
      the freedom that my generation wished for,
          the freedom that our queer elders and gay trailblazers dreamed up
            in the quiet temptations of generations
            in the isolation of closets and shadow
            in the Black trans women led riots of stonewall
            in the breaking apart of families
            in the death beds of AIDS lovers
            in the bright bold colors of the pride flag
        in the kisses, mouth to mouth, man to man, woman to woman,
      in the revolutions in film, poetry, art, music that named us real.
These movements line the path with scattered rainbow flowers
for this generation of queer kids to follow into their hopeful futures.
I love their hopeful futures, thinking of them grown up
and how the world will be better just because they are living in it.

I love their inability to be brought down by the outdated thinking of adults.
I love their inclusion and sensitivity.
I love their passion, their protest, their fight,
I love their loud brave voices demanding what's right.
I love that they are the fruits of so many trees,
        and that in each of their eyes, I see a little piece of me.

The Soul of Everything

the optometrist
and I sit in the dark
he shines
a beam
of light
through to the back
of my eye
I see
that I hold my own orbing planets
in these sockets

right retina
a jupiter swing
bending bright blue waves
to some dark space inside my head

left retina
its own violet Venus
in how she holds on to moving light

pathways unveiled
black holes turned inside out
to brilliance

and when he finishes
says the exam is over
I carry imprints
of two bright stars
burning
on my eyes
and everywhere I look   (light)
in faces   (light)
in trees   (light)
in a lifting bird   (light)
this new aura clouds my vision
as I move through the world

my windows
fully open
to the soul of everything

V.

TENDER AND ACHE

for Apis mellifera

Tender and ache, I am an exposed bloom,
a dandelion head with almost every wish blown away
still standing in an empty field with hope of fruiting a dream.

Can you see why I mother every possible thing?
Why the world becomes my womb and my hands a desperate sanctuary?

I rescued a bumble bee from between the window pane
and plastic sheeting of the greenhouse, a big bear of a bee,
fuzzy and stunned, on the brink of untimely death.
Who knows how long he waited for rescue. I cupped his slow body
in my hand and walked out to the lilac tree laden with blooms
and laid him inside a cluster of heavy-scented petals.
If you die, at least die happy inside here I said to him,
and his weakened bee arms clutched around the soft white flowers
as though he was hugging them so tightly,   then stillness.

I checked on him every hour while I gardened, and in a few hours
he buzzed by me on my way to the lilac—*I'm alive!*
a heavy song of thanks, a flight line of gratitude.

This is how I mother. I rock the smallest species to sleep,
lullaby our deepest human apologies into their innocent ears.

That same day, five million honeybees being shipped to Alaska
to pollinate orchards on ice shelves were rerouted by Delta airlines.
They waited on a hot tarmac in Atlanta for hours.
Hot-lanta! Record-breaking heat! The Weather Channel meteorologist joked.
The bees died in droves, lifeless yellow-black piles, bodies by the crateful,
eight hundred pounds of dead honeybees, an oversight, lost in the machinery
of luggage and transit, moved and left to swelter and starve.
Five millions bees and no lilacs to save them, no open hands,
no sweet petaled embrace, no song of forgiveness
whispered into their golden honeyed hives,
just the tragic end of five million precious, pollinating lives.

Tender and ache, my mother (nature) heart breaks
into five million pieces. I stand in a field and buzz with mourning.

Bombs Bursting in Air

everything is louder in a valley
and in our peaceful valley
it's days 'til the 4th
but the neighbors
have called in the artillery
have shot their rocket's red glare
to scare the shit out of our little dog

they shoot freedom into quiet forest air
at all hours of the day and night and day again
because this is *the country*
their country
    this is America damnit
    and we celebrate freedom
    with gunpowder and explosives

Layla is curled up in my arms shaking
and all of the birds have been singing different songs

on our evening walk
the bottle rockets and black cats attack us
flank us on all fronts   machine-gun   the soft dusk

pyrotechnics permeate the silence
with the lingering chaos of liberty
the ring of colonization

    I imagine my Vietnam vet father
    and the wars he brought home inside him
    stuffed into empty vodka bottles

    I imagine the children of Gaza, Ukraine, Syria, Gaza again
    with bombs as their lullabies
    their torn up skies their teared-up eyes

booms cacophony around our valley
as Layla shakes in my arms

bombs bursting in air
freedom's assaulting refrain

Flowers and Exit Wounds as America Celebrates "Independence" / Trigger Warning

I photograph flowers like a woman about to lose it all,
or one who already has. This July 4th—I don't celebrate,
feel the pang of autonomy and liberties
un-liberated from my body   my sisters' bodies.

So this morning, in my usual garden bed meandering,
watering from the front vegetable gardens to the back house gardens,
to the potted plants and the pollinator garden,
I photograph flowers up close, fill the frame with pincushion purple,
bright pink zinnia, blazing French marigolds,
coral geraniums, red ones too, white climbing jasmine,
dahlias and peonies, a bright golden sun with a thousand faces,
a photo of each one up close like a firework,
zoomed all the way in,
the petals spreading like sparks to the corners of my screen,
without the boom, without the bang
and the sulfur smell,
without scaring my little dog,
just silent beauty,
emanating its own vibration of light and color,
without the carnage of gunpowder.

The carnage of gunpowder—O, how bullets keep making their way
into my poems, how a 4th of July parade this morning
filled with marching bands and laughter suddenly became
another young adult white male with an AR-15 blasting holes indiscriminately
into bodies, carnage and bloodstain, screaming and panic-running,
flesh coagulating on the sidewalk on this independent morning.

The flowers. More flowers. I go outside to breathe,
to shake off the horror that will not shake off all of us,
the image of a toddler, a little boy named Aiden, wandering around the sidewalk
with blood on his little falling-down sock, his tiny tennis shoe.
Where are his parents? there's a viral twitter plea for help
to find his parents in all this chaos, all this continued chaos,
this every single fucking day chaos—
please, someone find his family,
please, America, what are we doing to our children?
please, Robb Elementary still rings with horror in my heart,

the screams of 19 children robbed of their futures,
and now this little boy, this little baby born in a pandemic,
is now an orphan, his parents blown apart at a parade, dead
in another American mass shooting.

The exit wound from the bullet of an AR-15
is the size of an orange—
It's like a grenade goes off inside them, said the trauma surgeon,
like slowly dragging your finger through water,
the bullet's energy and force
ripple outward at such a high speed
it makes the body a cavity of mangled flesh,
it blows it up from the inside,
and when these bullets are fired through children . . .

      no, don't write that line, Kai
      don't put that in the poem
      don't imagine it or name a thing so devastating

just go outside,
go outside and breathe,
get off twitter,
turn off the news,
take photographs of all the flowers
really close up,
closer,
even closer still,
fill your screen with petals and color—

when the fireworks explode independence tonight,
it's probably just

a gun.

No Choice

Since the supreme court land-grabbed our bodies back to 1973, I've been searching for wombs inside other lives, asking if they know they have more freedoms than human bodies who can carry a child. I scream inside the deep wells of certain flowers—purple columbine, golden bells, red hibiscus, a floating white lotus, all with their impervious blooming, their wildness, their capability to wither at the whim of wind. I google *female sex organ of a flower* and laugh at the irony of the word *pistil*, how a *pistil* in the flower kingdom carries an ovary and a stigma, a stigma that has no shame, but in the human names, an ovary has the stigma of men's desires and a pistol has less regulation than my womb. An AR-15 assault rifle in a classroom has more autonomy than the little girl it just blew bullets through. My heart keeps breaking at this country. I plead for light into the thousand faces of a mammoth sunflower, and they bow their pitying heads, set a thousand suns. I sit on my deck among the mourning doves cooing in the pine, and I too mourn what I thought was mine. This body. This skin and cells, this flesh, this bone. I am beyond mothering—know my body will never home or vessel a child, but this red state will bleed redder still with the trigger ban signatures of these scheming leaders, enforcing an unholy law that strips us all of our dignity and ability to do what is best for our own bodies. I scream into my valley and my mountains scream back. I clip my fingernails, and these little crescent moons ask me about ownership. Which cells of mine have been sold to the highest bidders? Which organs no longer do my own bidding? In two weeks, I will become Auntie Kai to a little girl, a niece who I cannot wait to meet, a sweet life who I have already met in my dreams, a new baby girl born into a world where she has more protection in her mother's womb now than she will when she comes out. Little girl, little girl, what is this world we have shaped for you when you have no choice to be born into it?

The Children of Gaza

This is a wailing in words for the children of Gaza—the children of Gaza with not enough gauze to bandage their wounds, to cover their eyes, to reattach their limbs. Did you know that the word gauze comes from Gaza, city of textiles and silk, city of strength? Now Gaza has no words left, no city. No words. No city. No words, only new acronyms like WCNSF, wounded child no surviving family. The children of Gaza have been buried under buildings, or laid next to mothers in mass graves, or eaten by animals because they couldn't be recovered from the streets, under nights of constant fire bombs. The children of Gaza are dying, are dead. 11,500+ children, 11,500+ little bright ones. Their limbs are not metaphors. Their splayed arms are not the branches of olive trees. Their eyes are not the seeds of lemons. Their cries are not the songs of freedom or liberation or hope. Their cries are just cries, they don't symbolize anything. No deeper meaning here, just that they wanted to be alive. Instantaneously gone. Evaporated by a barrage of bombs. Burned. Lost. Wiped out. Eradicated. Eliminated. Their small limp bodies are not metaphors, do not represent some greater cause. Their tears are just tears, negative space rivers pouring clean down their soot-covered cheeks, faces of dust and ash. I slipped in a metaphor there, **a river**, but the children of Gaza are still dead. They are silenced. They are bloody and broken. In pieces. Shards. They are covered by stones that were once a city. They are amputated and harshly stitched. The children of Gaza are bagged as the tiniest martyrs, names written on their arms in case they are found alive. Names buried. Families buried. Generations buried. Mothers mouths filled with ruby rubble dust and screaming. Premature babies are left to decompose in a firebombed hospital, still hooked up to dead machines. They needed life support so the nurses left them hooked up, but the nurses had to escape or be killed. Life support. What can support life here for the children of Gaza? Their families flee to the beaches only to be shelled by warships from the sea. The children of Gaza have nowhere to run. Nowhere to hide. Nowhere to escape. Only horror and destruction, only everything turned to memory or blackness. Only death and the smell of death. Their bodies are not metaphors. Nothing figurative about the language of this loss. Their small dead fingers point toward only their homeland laid to waste, they point at us asking *why didn't you stop this*, they point toward endings, not a future, not dreams, not laughter, not tomorrow. Dear little ones, Dear **souls of our souls**—I am sorry we've failed you. I am sorry that we could not make our bodies an iron dome above your skies, that your mothers' cries and fathers' hands could not shield you from the airstrikes, from the white phosphorus breathing into your lungs as you screamed your last breaths, from the genocide of your people filling the streets with blood. There are no metaphors here. Dear children of Gaza—beautiful living ghosts, beautiful dead ghosts. We weep for you. We weep for you. You are our children.

All children are our children. May all beings know peace.

Bird Man Releases 115th Eagle

for Haliaeetus leucocephalus *and Tommy Young*

There's 10,000 pounds per square inch in that six-inch foot
that you don't want to get into—no man in the world can even get one toe
of that open if it gets hold of you! Tommy shouts to the crowd
from the bed of an old pickup truck backed up to a mountain vista's blue expanse.

The sun setting is a halo behind his head.
       Tommy's been rehabilitating eagles
       and other wildlife since he was a little boy,
       knew no other way because his parents did the same,
       bolts and screws in his vertebrae
       after a 30-foot fall from a tree
       trying to help a parliament of baby owls,
and here he is now—another mountaintop of hope realized
and this 115th injured eagle he's named Liberty will once again fly
with wings open wide against the great open sky.

Liberty was found months ago, wing dragging on the ground and injured,
talon marks of another eagle shredded through his flesh
from mid-flight battle or dangerous courtship dance.

Today, Liberty flies again.

I'll hold him for as long as I can so that y'all can see his eyes,
but I've also had my lip nearly torn off so I've got to lean waaaaay back.

Hooded, Liberty is clutched close to Tommy's chest,
       I wonder how Tommy's heartbeat pounds calmness to him.
Liberty is tense but docile as he is unshackled
from leather jesses by another master falconer—
a deep trust between the two men.
Tommy's hands hold firm around Liberty's legs
protecting the falconer from certain bloodletting if talons take hold.

How is it that there can be so much courage—
to hold such an unfathomable vice-grip predator
in human hands and not think there is some grace,
some shared understanding between species,
at least in this moment?

As soon as the jesses are undone and hood swiftly removed
Liberty sees the sky,
Liberty feels the pull of clouds,
Liberty's golden talons unfurl like gaping mouths,
and Tommy's heart pounds *almost almost almost* into Liberty's feathers,
his eyes dart around taking in the human awe.

He's so beautiful a little girl's voice raises above the crowd.
Tommy turns to face the open sky over the lake
                    Alright Dad, this one's for you!
and in one breath's   e x h a l a t i o n
as if wind
as if updraft
as if crosscurrent to the supernatural
Liberty's wings span their fullest potential and he is   weightless,
he is sky   blue   wind   air   flight   antigravity   and   soaring
onlookers *oooooh* and *aaaaah*
as Liberty shifts quick and follows the tree-line
in a trajectory of gratitude across Tommy's tearful eyes.

Come back, Brother! he shouts.
The crowd chuckles,

I know he means it.   Brother.

It's the 4th of July and I could metaphor this moment to death,
with America *this* and bald eagle *that*,
but better this be just about one good man,
a man who rehabs bobcats, bears, foxes, pumas, panthers,
a man who released the 115th injured eagle from his healing hands,
a man who gathers people on mountaintops
so for just
a split second
they can truly experience

freedom.

SHADOW

for Felis catus

We have been feeding him for three years now—a black feral cat with jade eyes and golden irises and long wizard whiskers, who we've affectionately named Shadow. First she appeared as a mirage, a puff of smoke moving quickly through the forest on the other side of the backyard pond, a trick of the eye, a hallucination. Never a bad omen, a superstition, or a witch's sidekick, unless you think of us as witches—in that case, I have another poem to write entirely. For years, Shadow lingered on the property peacefully. Sure, there were a few chased birds, caught birds, feathers strewn across wet grass, but most days she would sit and stare at us from a hundred yards out, silent watcher, wondering about us, watching the dance of our lives. He crept close and closer as the months moved into years. She would sleep on the huge stump of the tree we fell in the garden, sun rising on her round body curled on her grand wooden throne, black fur rusting in morning light. I'd coo through the window. *Reader, I know you notice the pronouns switching from he to she, but we have never gotten close to enough to really tell if Shadow is a boy or a girl.* They are just Shadow, non-binary cat, untouchable, a flash. Three years of this gender ambiguity. Three years of detachment, but still loving. Three years of feeding in the morning and evening. Three years of *I guess Shadow is our cat now,* though sometimes we do notice he saunters over from the neighbor's with a fat full belly. No judgment here. Get your kicks, cat. Take what the world is serving, wild one. Three years of *psssss psssss psssss psssss* and hitting a fork to the little ceramic plate we leave on the deck for her. Shadow runs up from under the house, from one of his hiding spaces, or from the cush luxury cabana that my wife built so he could survive winters outside. He meows and gets almost close enough to touch, but still aloof, jumpy, won't allow a single hair to be stroked, scurries, backs away until we are a safe distance. I know he'd *like* to be loved, would enjoy a cuddle or belly rub, would see that our calves and ankles are great to rub against, but there is always that unbreakable wild he holds onto, the feral that's helped him stay alive. Just because you have never touched something, it can still be proclaimed beloved, it can still fall into dependent. We still add her kitty kibble and canned delicacies to the groceries each week. We aren't *really* cat people. You know of the loyalty we have to our dogs, and yes, Layla gives Shadow a run for his money around the garden, black dog chasing black cat, mirrors running from their reflections. But let's go ahead and make this official. *Reader, we have a cat—*a feral black beautiful sleek creature who lounges on our deck in summer's long afternoons, who sits on our porch at dusk by the big red pot that holds the coral honeysuckle vines, and delights for hours in watching the hummingbirds dip and whirr in her sightline, bouncing from bloom to bloom. She doesn't jump or lunge toward them with fangs gleaming, just sits in stillness, head turning with curious angles of appreciation. Our Shadow—fed and sleepy and home.

Psssss psssss psssss psssss.

Do You Want to Play Outside?

I can't with all these apocalypses intersecting right now—
there is a steady flow of bad news
that tips the tipping point even tippier
into doom, and I only want to stare at the red star hibiscus
newly in bloom outside the kitchen window,
leave the dishes and go out into the garden,
dance with its dinner-plate-sized face
to a place far away from here,
dissociate from this humanness
long enough to associate again with the wild,
find my inner child
who had to grow up much too fast,
take her small hand in mine
and show her the wonder of the glasshouse spider
in the greenhouse wrapping up a metallic bright blue wasp
in a swaddle of silk, and how its body looks like a cradled baby, loved
even in death—the spider and the wasp, a mutual understanding.
Yes, look and see how this is a part of greater things,
little child, we can search out the beauty of things before
and even after they've died.

Look at our beautiful breaking world. It gets so hard, doesn't it?
We can still search out the wonder, can't we?
Find that hope is a language spoken by wildfire-scorched redwood forest floors,
how seeds are genetically designed to just keep striving toward the light,
to keep pushing and pushing through the darkening earth
into some new possibility of reaching,
here—
I am reaching,
pushing against the darkening earth.

I want to carve out a space for my tender heart to still have
a place to get on my knees in awe
of a small wild thing,
> *let the soft animal of my body love what it loves,*
and that is this—
anthropomorphizing the spiders and the bees,
the flowers and the trees, their blossoms and seeds
into something that holds me in all the breaking.

I am pushing against the darkening of these laws, 890 new Arkansas laws
pushed out by a legislative session with only cruel intentions to harm

the trans kids, the gays, the Black and the Brown,
to find some new ways to keep the already downtrodden down,
to erase history from the consciousness of babes,
to revisionist the stories of America being built by the enslaved,
school teachers speaking through republican red tape
duct tape silver linings over their mouths dressed as a $50K pay raise,
and we cannot just stand by and be complicit with our silence,
we cannot seek to build a better world
while witnessing whitewashing bigotry and violence,
but how do we fight against a darkening world?

How do we fight against a darkening world?
I'm asking, sincerely.
How?

The pile-ons keep piling on and honestly all I can do
is sing a sweet tender song
to our koi fish swimming in their pond,
they know not of our silly human struggles,
they just swim in their beautiful circles impervious to our pains.
All I can do is bring my inner child to the lip of the water
and show her the colors of their golden slick bodies
glinting the light of morning in slants of sun.

All I can do is have my inner child
find my mother's inner child
and ask her if she wants to go play outside,
take her on a walk through the greening forest
and lift up the understories of trees with our small hands,
get soil on the soles of barefoot feet
and walk through the healing of generational trauma.

Maybe that's the answer, this small world, this ripple of influence,
these beautiful circles in which we swim around
feeling each others pains—
maybe if we take each other's hands,
if our inner children could find each other again
       before the maddening of adulthood,
       before the cynicism of growth,
       before the ache of aging,
maybe if we just knocked on each other's doors and asked sincerely—

     Hey, do you want to play outside with me?

AMBER

for Ficus carica

It's golden hour in our valley, and I walk through
late summer's dry grass to our fig tree,
peek under yellowing leaves in search of
the heavy sweetness hanging purple and thick.

Like the smallest leather punching bags, I find them
one by one, ready, weighted with their honeyed song,
rouged with the bruising of being made
ripe in the shortening days.

There is no tug needed from my fingers
as I find each laden fruit—
each fig waits to fall into my hands.

Through their soft skin bottoms,
tiny amber droplets of candied nectar
harden in the crisp autumnal air,
and when I hold one up against the backdrop
of the setting sunshine, a halo of amber light hugs
the shadowed underbelly sticky and plump in my palm.

Is anyone else noticing this level of intrinsic beauty right now?
Who else is holding a fig up to the sun,
caught in the amber droplets of decadence
radiant with heliotropic breath?

> *I must name this sweetness as the world*
> *burns, must hold it in the memory of words.*

I bring the supple handful up to my love,
this bounty of palpable pleasure—three for her, three for me.

We bite into their supple dark flesh,
suck and crunch the tiny seeds,
rush of honey, natural sugars,
textures of collapsible summer rain,
an earth of seasons held in a silken bag,
like tasting each other
again
for the first time.

Catalog of Receiving

after Rebecca Lindenberg

You give me wildflowers planted from seed, standing high as our heads now.
You give me bees tangled in their colors, today's late autumn.

You give me season after season, growing gardens and shaping land.
You give me not enough time to grow old with you, to fine wine beside you.

You give me ripe persimmon, cinnamon toast, licorice tea, eucalyptus.
You give me sweetness. And bitters.

You give me a tattered luna moth and say *don't put it in the cabinet of wonders*.
You give me a smile when I put it in there anyway.

You give me a cabinet of wonders, curiosity under warm light glow,
metallic beetles and feathers, quartz crystal, jewels, and bone.

You give me honey whiskey straight up and slow dances,
even last night, how we have learned to lead and follow after all these years.

You give me The Beatles, Cat Stevens, Bob Dylan, Joni Mitchell, everything blue.
You give me your eyes, my everything, blue.

You give me oil paintings stained with your hours, visions of striving,
a new school of thought, ancient as time, your face in every line.

You give me hot vegetable soup made fresh this morning.
You give me morning, and mourning.

You give me meteor showers outside on a blanket. You give me stars
falling out of the sky and into our mouths, glossing our lips.

You give me triggers and battles and broken glass.
You give me armor chiseled off in moonlight, glinting in dewey grass.
You give me vex, and hex, and sex, and feeling beautiful naked finally.

You give me dry earth and oceans, deserts painted with fire.
You give me sequoias and giant redwoods and ancient bristlecones.
You give me tears of reverence as we walk in a scorched forest hand in hand.

You give me your heart of Light. You give me family. You give me home.
You give me tomorrow and tomorrow and tomorrow, holding today.

Monarch Mama, in Five Stages

for Danaus plexippus

Midwifing sixteen Monarch caterpillars for a couple weeks now,
I've watched them grow from half a centimeter to five times that,
molting into bigger, thicker selves. With each instar of the larval stage,
shedding old selves and becoming newer, stronger, longer
as though transforming is their only job—
well that, and eating the fresh milkweed bundles I bring into their netted enclosure
safe from the elements, smack dab in the middle of our living room.

These temporary residents of change, poster boys for transformation,
yellow-black-white striped little horses of hunger—*reader, I'm invested.*

In their first few days, they were so minuscule,
now they're gluttonous machines of internal greening,
this miraculous process that no one teaches them
yet they all adhere to, their metamorphic religion, to grow and grow,
shed and shed, eat and shit, eat and shit, and grow some more
until finally they climb up to higher ground to do God's work—
not the god of man, but the real God, that incomprehensible force
that says you can strip every part of yourself away and begin again
as an entirely new flying thing.

* * * * *

Tonight, from the top of the enclosure,
the first of the fifteen cats **J**s from spun silk into a hanging last dance,
a **J** form that soon will contract and shrink with some inexplicable alchemy.
Her skin will split from the back of her head and accordion a black exoskeleton
up to the silk rope she wove—the only tie back to her old self.
She'll wiggle 'til that old form falls away, to finally reveal the chrysalis.
I can't wait to see it. It's disgusting and wonderful, mysterious and unbelievable.
I stare at the silhouette of the **J** for far too long, for science,
like watching paint dry, like a watched pot never boils,
like a child staring up the chimney expecting some red suit miracle,
and the **J** hangs there in her silence, clinging to the promise of butterfly.

* * * * *

And just like that, *of course,* when I run out of the room for a second,
I come back and the hanging **J** is now a chrysalis, jewel of shiny bright green,
a long orb of new life almost neon in its greenness, as though

all the hungry bites of milkweed through insatiable typewriter mouth
have turned a belly of leaves inside out to bloom here,
little royal thing—with her golden chrysalis crown
of metallic iridescent pigmented cells,
gold dots through which oxygen now flows,
golden heart creating itself inside there, I'm sure,
bright wings forming through the unfathomable mystery.

* * * * *

Fourteen days later, emergence. All fifteen little green gems
have blackened to transparency, orange and black wing colors
show through the veil that thins into metamorphosis, and finally
after all these days of stillness, there is movement   a stirring   a waking up
from extended sleep, a reincarnation of sorts, and each chrysalis becomes
a butterfly, a whole new being emerges from the forty-wink fortnight
of transformation and drops from a hatch upside-down, holding on with new legs,
as bright wings unfold and life is pumped through—my God, they're just beautiful.

> *Hush little royals, don't you cry,*
> *Mama's going to lift you to the sky.*
> > *Emerge from your chrysalis, dry your wings,*
> > *rock back and forth now while I sing.*
> *Hush little monarchs, you're safe here,*
> *the wild world will hold you, don't you fear.*
> > *I've watched you grow and I've held you dear,*
> > *your migration starts when the skies are clear.*
> *And when that beautiful sky turns blue*
> *I'll smell the flowers and think of you.*
> > *Hush my sweet baby butterflies,*
> > *Mama's going to lift you to the skies.*
> *And when the winds carry you then you'll know*
> *my heart goes with you, wherever you go.*

* * * * *

Reader, I'm empty nesting now, still tiptoeing through the house soft-voiced so as not
to disturb the monarchs, their sensitivity to light and sound, their wild growing, though
they've long flown the coop to warmer climes. They've left me with this—*When you do
finally break out of that form for the last time, escape the chrysalis of your own becoming,
yes, hang there for a moment, dry your new wings, feel that new you pumping with life,
then fly off and never, ever look back.*

Emerge.

EXPECTING PERSIMMONS

for Diospyros kaki Fuyu

Every year for the last three years, when autumn cusps the edges of summer
there comes a large flat-rate USPS box heavy and weighted,
stuffed and swollen with glowing suns.

My mother mails fruit—not a mixture, not something that spoils in transit,
but crisp and fresh, firm and taut, a plump bounty of Japanese persimmons,
their sunlight skin shiny and strong, leaving room for ripening,
leaving time for eating between me and my love.

Dozens of little orange planets
I fill into our biggest fruit bowl. They spill out   over   the   edges
and onto the kitchen island as we laugh and slice one open,
the juice pooling with our gratitude,
          how can we ever eat all these persimmons
turned gifts   turned meals   turned tangible expression
of a mother's love stretching out over the miles,
spilling gold all over our house,
a hundred suns rising in the morning pouring their light into dark corners.

My mother always loved in food, expressed herself in morsel to mouth
not words, but the flavors of her love to savor the colors of her heart,
and I guess I should count myself lucky for the extra weight
I've always carried around because it means I was loved,
it means I was cared for in another language.

It's been two weeks now since the laden bright box of persimmons
filled our mailbox, and tonight I cut slices for my students
at the adult writing workshop I teach,
and they are still so sweet, softening with time (*as we do*)
and I have told the story year after year of my little Filipino mother
stuffing as many persimmons as she can fit into that flat rate box,
and we pass around the plate of fruit, crunching and savoring sweet swallows,
and each student takes one home—persimmons on the move
in bags, jacket pockets, once-empty hands,
and in the morning, each will have
a sunrise
creating slants of light
from inside their kitchens,
a mother's love   spilling over
in gold.

WILL YOU WATCH ME PLAY NINTENDO?

for Alexander

Alexander, Prince of Smiles—you are now in the
will you watch me play Nintendo?
phase of your growing, six-and-three-quarters years old,
with the tenderness of an old soul and the raucous of boyhood
swirled into your 44-pound little body.

Of course I want to watch you play Nintendo—
yes, dive me into Super Mario's 3D world and show me
how to swirl into power stars and jump over toadstools,
because I want you to know anything that matters to you,
dear boy, also matters to me.

Auntie Kai will *definitely* play with your sticky green slime
spilled out from a cracked open plastic dinosaur egg.
I'll even show you how to hold it in your hand
and fake sneeze out a wad of slimy green boogers
dripping from your tiny fingers, because I am fluent
in the language of little boys and funny faces—
I know the fascination with *butt* and *poop* and *fart* will pass.
I know, too, that laughter translates into I love you.

I want to build something with you (a foundation that lasts)
so yes, I will pull out your thousands of Legos,
your Gravitrax and blocks, your Magnatiles and Magformers
and build a sprawling village together
because that's what it takes to raise a child.
And darling boy, I will always be another home for you—
a wild open heart inside your house,
a strong wall you can lean on,
a foundation unshakable for your feet.

I'll even stand by willingly, despite my inner love for the purity of colors,
as you mix the bright teal, white unicorn sprinkle, and deep violet
play-dough colors into one big ball of hideous grey,
because sweet boy, if this is how you play,
never let me stand in your way,
your creativity sings music into my childless bones.

And when bedtime comes
and all you want is me to carry you

like a potato sack up to bed
and read you stories of Daniel Tiger and dinosaurs,
I am gladly the escort of your dreams.
We snuggle and talk about school and feelings.
We laugh about quiet, silly things.
You wrap your little body into mine
and inside I ache for what I am missing,
but you, dear child, give me the sweetest glimpse
into the intimacy of *mother*.

Perhaps you'll never know what it means to me
when you wake up in the middle of the night
and realize I am still sleeping beside you,
the glow-in-the-dark stars on your blue
curtains still emanating soft light,
you put your drowsy hand on my cheek
and whisper *I love you—*
what unreached chambers of my heart
suddenly open and flood with your tenderness.

The next day at the Mexican restaurant when you're cold
I take you outside and we giggle as we do
six-and-three-quarters jumping jacks in the blazing sun,
and when you climb back into my lap at the table
you turn to me and say
Too bad you don't have any kids, Auntie Kai, you'd be a good mom.

I try not to cry because I know
I still mother
every little life I can touch,
every animal, bird, bug, plant, flower,
every heart I can reach with my tender power,
every single classroom child,
every Alexander, Prince of Smiles.

It's Not That I Can't Have Children

It's not that I can't *have* children
that my body is not a house—
it's just that my life
never had the chance to make room,
did not open in a way to make itself a womb,
the timing of years between my lover and mine,
the age of different periods of mothering inclining
and declining at the same time.

There just was never the solid enough ground of myself
or the chance even,
a man
was not in the cards,
and I never even played from that deck,
so it never really became
a possibility,
and I am almost at the apex of this want,
this deep yearning to hold a child of my own flesh and bone,
to make my body a home—

but perhaps that proverbial ship has sailed,
and the life that I have created
is the life I have   the life I love.
Perhaps my womb has turned outwards somehow,
and my heart is fertility itself.

Perhaps I have always been a mother
without a human child,
searching for my children in the trees,
in the understory of ancient forests,
hidden under smooth stones,
in warm fur-covered bodies,
in wing tuft and claw,
in the exoskeletons of nymphs,
phylums that lack a sort of mothering I can give,
and so I tend to the wild ones,
I mother other kingdoms,
rock every other species to sleep—
the green and howl and pulse and bloom.

It's not that I can't *have* children,
it's that I already do.

WAITING FOR A LETTER

for Genghis Infinity, April 22, 2008–November 14, 2022

but no postman will come,
no amazon delivery of your warm body back to me.

Didion named it *wishful psychosis,*
some magical thinking and hallucination,
this waiting for a sign, but I speak in subtle worlds—
I see the imprints of your atoms in the swirl of days,
I feel you here in how the birds sing,
how the backyard pond spills over into stream,
and lately you have been coming to see me in my dreams.

Waiting for a letter, a sign, a way to rewind time,
phantasms of light and shape that shape the body of my ache,
waiting for your face to appear again from behind the ash,
in the stones and branches of moving trees,
a letter never comes, except the letter G,
little darling one, won't you please come back to me?

There were no words that told me farewell,
nothing spoken from your mouth or written by your hands,
just the faded stars blooming in your eyes as you died in my arms,
the fixed and dilated sky I cry my mothering into,
always on the cusp of watershed,
I move slow into these new emptier days.

A being is a being is a being of light,
and the world cannot weigh the validity of my grief,
if you are the only son I ever knew.

I am waiting for a letter.
I am waiting for all the wondrous letters to return to me,
waiting for the whole alphabet to form into words other than loss,
but for now, every letter spells your missing name, like water,
my poems gravity-flow into the you-shaped hole that spreads in my chest,
my sounds reflect only the cosmic distance   yet you still shine   in me.
I am waiting for my letters to shift into the memory of all our joy,
and the time will come when this love language sings another song,
but for now, I will write the dirges.

All the letters, G.

Is This Grief?

Tomorrow, it will be one month without you
and I swear, it has rained grey white fog mist storm for weeks,
like every cell around us weeps since you've gone.

It's been hard to go on with the holidays
but it's like an unspoken thing between all of us that it brings you here—
if we hang up as many twinkling lights through the house as we can,
maybe the emptiness and cold will fill with the warmth
of making light out of this dark—everything is colored with you.

Have you become a star, my puppalito, my sunny bonanza,
or are you even bigger, more vast, temporary visiting universe?
Have you returned to your place in the cosmos, sweet boy?
Forgive me for wanting you back in my arms, sleeping on my chest,
the weight of you missing has me unhinged from the ground of myself,
has me floating in an unknown lonely sky.

Did I tell you enough how much I love you?
Did I show you enough my thankful heart, my open arms?
Did I name myself mother for you to be my only son?

Gentle boy, Little Big Heart, please be wherever you need to be,
comet, star, universe, infinity, but also please   somehow stay close to me,
show your face in the clouds and stone, manifest that warmth for me.
I've been standing in the face of the sun to feel you with my eyes closed.
I think of you, I speak your name, and I'm painted with brushstrokes of gold.

Forgive me for not scattering your ashes all over our land,
I want to keep every particle of you close and whole,
this is selfish I know—it's only been a month since you've gone
and I'm still doing everything I can to hold on.
          Is this grief?   Am I doing it wrong?
Are you teaching me even how to move through this, sweet Spirit Fu?

These days are long though it is winter. The fire is embered, waiting for breath.
I am still breathing and sometimes I can still feel you, your lion heart.

We are of different worlds now, two kingdoms, two planes,
but my dear beautiful sweet best good boy, Genghis . . .
love has no other name.

SOLSTICE INSIDE

It's the winter solstice,
the shortest day of the year,
the longest night,
the darkest of all darks
bending somehow back toward light.
I want to write a new poem,
a poem that brings the darkness of my lack of words
back into some space of light
but try as I might, nothing comes.
It's like language died with my dog,
or that grief is a language I don't speak fluently
so writing feels foreign and upside-down,
feels like an abandoned mother
tongue that I can't wrap my words around,
so all I hear is the sound
of stars
breaking
with their light.

The sun hangs invisible on this solstice night
at its highest or lowest point in the sky,
seated at the Tropic of Capricorn,
my January 1st birth sign,
and the goat in me wants to stop
looking for the next mountain to climb.
Every bone in my body is tired.
There has been a shift in my hips
and my legs want to stand still where I am,
or lay down, or find a goat cave to hibernate in
until all this dark becomes something I can swallow down,
alchemize it all into gold like I used to when I was stronger, younger,
but now the days and nights just seem to get longer and longer
still, the tears
keep welling up in my throat,
pool in the corners of my eyes,
shape my smile into something that I don't recognize in the mirror.

I beg for a solstice inside,
the long night to teach me something about growth and letting go,
the short day to teach me that every minute is precious,
my bones, my cells, my arms, my legs, my heart
to bend somehow back toward light.

SELF-PORTRAIT AS GREENHOUSE

There were never really walls in the first place,
just antique window panes cobbled together
in the shape of a house, leaning against a bigger house,
but it could hold the few hours of south-facing light well enough,
it was warm enough   until it wasn't.

Plastic sheeting, thick and double-lined, hung for added insulation
made the string of Christmas lights inside glow golden in a frosted incandescence—
to onlookers walking by it appeared to shine from within.
All the precious plants were placed safely inside at the turn of seasons,
the bird of paradise with her wings spread wide,
the night-blooming cereus cusping her first flowers,
the prayer plant, purple queen, and purple wood sorrels,
the strange little succulents,
sword ferns, and geraniums,
the budding fig trees and red maples,
flowers and seeds and dreams of spring.

With the smallest threat of November cold,
the makeshift greenhouse withstood with its warm embrace,
shielding the tender wild ones from winter,
an everlasting summer next to a space heater and her care,
until the December winter storm weathermen called
once in a generation blanketed the country,
until the usual tolerable temperatures
became a deathly dangerous flash freeze phenomenon—
-16 degree windchill paired with the naïveté
that this pieced-together pretty twinkling thing
could keep out the fingers of frigid death,
could lock out encroaching encasement in ice.

Meager cobbled windows were not enough,
the small space heater was a chuckle of irony,
and all the precious greening things froze solid by morning,
leaves shattering like broken glass,
the water in their cells frozen and ruptured,
tissues irreversibly damaged beyond repair.
No amount of sunshine could thaw the imminent.
No amount of shuffling them inside after the fact
could reverse nature's cold cruel hand,
nothing salvageable, just a garden
of beautiful death.

For days, the corpses of trees
stood like soldiers left to fight in a forgotten war,
the greenhouse now a graveyard
of more grief.

God, it's been a hard year.

Maybe this metaphor is going too far—
I am looking at myself as this cobbled-together greenhouse
of warmth, of light, of protection for tender growing things,
and *once in a lifetime,*
the cold escapes inward through the permeable cracks,
the body finally knows that nothing can hold back the dying,
the walls are still not really walls
but windows
that are trying still to let the light in,
and for now,
what shines inside is the memory of life,
what glows is all the ache,
the promise of eternal summer
unkept.

In the corner of the greenhouse, there are still seeds
quietly sleeping in brown paper bags
labeled *marigold, milkweed, hummingbird vine, giant zinnia, thistle,*
and maybe the flash freeze death
barely kissed
their little heads.

In the darkness of these unforgiving days,
I learn that nature is all about cycles and loss, though life always goes on.

Sometimes winter comes in fast and hard in unforeseeable ways,
and the structure you stand as yourself
falls woefully unprepared.

Yet still, you renew your identity as a house of windows.

Inside, all the green and tender things might unavoidably die—
but you cut off the dead branches and start over
from bare root or broken bulb, a promise
that some day there will be a rebirth
of spring.

MY SON FLOWERS

My son flowers
in different ways now that he's dead,
gone now a year, but still always here,
his life blooms in the way that the sun falls upon leaves
and shines gold through each breeze-waving green.

My son flowers
in the facades of chipped stones
      scattered around our land like monuments carved by his spirit,
      lion, dragon, dog—immovable boulders that stay here, present.

My son flowers
in the shadows of bark on white oak trees,
      his face silhouetted in the strips of time
      weathered to feather into the appearance of his eyes.

He is permeating worlds to let me know,
that though he travels in a different form, he is
still beside me, wherever I go—
I feel him every time it rains or when the wind blows.

My son flowers
in all the growing things, the blossoms this year
seemed to be more colorful, the wildflowers even wilder,
the garden soil richer, the trees reaching higher,
up to some other world where he watches like a sentinel of joy.

My Genghis, my little boy.
Despite what the world says about sons and daughters
only being human, my son flowers.

We meet at the veil some nights,
lift a cloak of stars, cross back and forth over rainbow bridges,
move through dimensions and cross lateral planes,
I just have to close my eyes, just have to say his name.

My grief has transformed into transcendence,
into knowing he's always here.
He's taught me how I will navigating future griefs—
how living with a loved one's spirit is its own relief.

My son flowers
through the seasons—
           in the sun bright blinding warm light of summer,
           I bask in the glow of otherworldly radiance, son shine,

in the way that each fall leaf spirals down from the branch,
and its own individual song reverberates a howl of him,

           in the winter emptiness and cold, in the ice and snow,
           his heart is the hearth of our fireplace glow,

in the beginning again of spring,
he blooms in the unbroken promise of everything.

In the Path of Totality, Umbral Illumination (April 8, 2024)

The sun kissed me good morning today,
bright face peeking up
from behind mountains of tall pine,
mirrored in silent lake glass
as if to say to me—*look, today is the day my heart becomes yours.*

I walk wide-eyed in morning grass
laced with dew universes and intricate greening.
I press the soft wet earth between my toes,
forgive my flawed human vessel
and feel my chest rise toward the open sky
as if to say to the sun—*look, today is the day my heart becomes yours.*

The sun readies her body of fire and gold for a slow dance with our moon,
a planetary tango of time and space, orbits and penumbras, shadow and light.

A line that divides our country
will bring it back together again in celestial beauty,
millions of darkened eyes pointed to sky witnessing wonder
as the sun folds light into herself to reveal
a diamond ring   a crown.

The total solar eclipse is moments away and I can feel us spinning toward her.
My body moves in waves if I lie still enough to become an ocean.
I close my eyes and feel the tug of tides moon-rise inside me.
My imagination senses a shadow
move across my face, everything goes dark,
my cheeks blush red and burn with the anticipation of totality.

Glorious sun—make me a silhouette you can turn back into stars,
the cosmos inside me is rising to meet you.

We are poised to marry the sun today,
a total solar eclipse dance
in the umbra of Hot Springs National Park,
waiting to make light out of darkness in the middle of the day.

We're watching the heavens-in-waiting from a carved out personal sky,
a circle of ancient friends drinking ancient waters revolving here in love—
we turn around to see ourselves becoming infinite again,
we bow to the Gods we see in each other   behind our human forms,

we follow our own shadows to the glow of our beginnings—
our smiles are solar eclipse sun salutations,
our eyes are ever-shooting stars,
our hearts lead us only to light unfolding   into more light.

Let's use this celestial moment in universal time.

Use this day to eclipse
the moments you want to leave behind.

See your own personal Path and Totality today,
your own unique world of wholeness,
the perfect swirling universe of you.

See that you have everything you need already inside you.

Kiss the journey below your own perfect feet,
your feet that brought you to this perfect moment.

You are holy.

     You are sacred.

         You are enough.

You are poised to marry the eclipsing sun today.
She already kissed you good morning.
Through your dark glasses, you can see her curves merging and bending,
transcending our earthly measurements to reach a cosmic climax.

Look around. Look up. Breathe.

When the sun offers you a diamond ring today—
when she gets down on one blazing knee
and asks if you want to let your dark shadows pass over and through,

look up with your open heart to her
bright eclipsing reflection

and say
    I do.

        I do.

           I do.

Forgive Me

for the Poets through the Pandemic

Forgive me if I stare too long
at the way light bends
around your cheekbones and neck,
at how your hair falls
just so sweetly over your eyes
or how you tuck it behind your ear
nervously when you speak.

Forgive me if I don't speak,
or if my words trip over my tongue
trying to tell you thank you—
I love you—
you saved me—
I've waited so long—
I didn't know what I was waiting for
but here you are—

so forgive me if I stare too long.
I've never seen this side of you before,
there in your flesh and wholeness,
in your perfect you-shaped everything
for me to finally see
and be next to
in my me-shaped everything,
our survival-prone bodies
and poem-hungry hearts
who clung to each other
like moons,
like refuge,
like safe harbor.

I swear your words life-rafted me through
that day, week, those months, years
and now we are here,
so forgive me if I stare too long,
if I get lost in the song of our conversation
because I keep focusing on your mouth,
on the light glinting off your teeth,
on your smile in real time.

What does your unrehearsed voice
sound like in casual tones?
In laughter?
How does it echo in the atoms around us?
How does your humanity
permeate the space?
I am hungry for more than
your sound bites and heart emojis—
I want the raw uncut wonder of you,
glimmering human, I call friend.

So forgive me in advance if my hug
holds on too tight,
if it reaches beyond
the customary hug time
into bones settling,
into heartbeats syncing,
into sinking into you
after all this almost drowning.

Forgive me if my tears drizzle your shoulder,
here, you can have my shoulder, too.
We've been carrying so much haven't we?
Yes, I know he died,
she died,
you're still recovering,
your body still aches,
you're so scared,
I know it's over,
she's gone,
I know I know
the bombs the bombs the bombs
and the children
won't stop growing
into this broken world
and it's all too much, isn't it, my dear poet?

Haven't our pens bled new shades of grief?

So forgive me if I reach
for your hand this time in much realer life,
liquid crystal screens faded
into tangible bodies,
skin, fingers, and palms,
forgive me if my cells dance in small ecstasies at the touch of you,

I promise it's only all this pent-up longing
for humanity, for community,
for closeness and friends,
for kindred hearts coming to the end
of a catastrophic time,
before we begin another—

Forgive me if I try, in my naïve way,
to stop this moment in time and hold onto you.
Forgive me if my heart weeps and sings
in this dance of joy and fleeting.
Forgive me for greeting you
with everything I have—
I didn't mean to make it weird,
but life gets shorter and shorter the longer we stand here,
but let's stand here,
really stand in this moment,
let's look around at this family we built in the dark,
see how the light bends around
and through us all,
together
in our glorious bodies,
our wondrous shoulders,
our open hands,
open hearts,

and forgive me if I stare too long—

you are just so beautiful.

Coming to a Poem Again

There are many ways to come to a poem again—

When you feel broken in two,
step silently toward the page as if it is something you can fall into,
heart first, then hands, open and waiting,
pressing cheekbone to the blankness asking *am I still here?*

Then listen. Wait.

You have walked through fallow fields,
hours, days, weeks, months without words,
but they've never been gone, not truly,
their sounds just move in different songs,
perhaps in color, perhaps shadow and light,
perhaps a flight in the trees, or in a drop of dew,
the words you cling to still also cling to you.

Silence speaks. And time.

Listen. Wait.

Realize you are the language.
The fertile ground is your own wild life.

The poem is your breath,
your heartbeat,
your heart

returning returning returning

to the page—

to a poem—

Acknowledgments

The author would like to thank the hardworking editors and staff of the following publications, literary journals, and anthologies in which versions of these poems have previously appeared.

About Place Journal (Black Earth Institute): "Ode to the Hornworm"

ALOCASIA: "Night Blooming Cereus / Queen of the Night" and "Amber"

Amethyst Review: "The Soul of Everything"

Anti-Heroin Chic: "Just Talk"

Arkana Magazine: "Shadow" and "It's Not That I Can't Have Children"

Bottlecap Press: "Without Saying it, a Poem About the *"

Blue Heron Review: "I Sit with a Master"

CUTTHROAT, A Journal of The Arts: "Coming to a Poem"

EKL Review: "Waiting for a Letter"

Elysium Review: "Lesbian Flower"

Eunoia Review: "Self-Portrait as Greenhouse"

For the Sonorous: "Ode to Ramen Noodles"

Lavender Review: "As You Stand in a Field of Diamonds, I Follow You in a Poem"

Lily Poetry Review: "Midwifing Tadpoles in the Anthropocene"

Luna Luna Magazine: "Keys"

Mystic Illuminations: "Petals"

Pirene's Fountain: "Crashing Toward Light"

Prairie Schooner: "Clutch"

Sage Cigarettes Magazine: "Aerial Caterpillar Ballet," "Unicorn," and "Beyond Us"

Slant: A Journal of Poetry: "Thirst"

Still: The Journal: "No Choice," "Expecting Persimmons," and "Black Snake"

Terrain.org: "In the Path of Totality, Umbral Illumination"

The Night Heron Barks: "I Screenshot a Woman on Zoom"

YES, Poetry: "A Star with My Brown Eyes"

My Gratitude

It is always **you** who I thank first, dear Reader. Thank you for moving through this collection with me and making it to this point where I can speak to you in clear-eyed gratitude. Thank you for holding space for my poems in your heart. Thank you for the images that shaped in your mind as you read, the vibrations and thoughts that were projected as you moved through the collection. These are some of my most vulnerable poems, and I am grateful to have had them in your hands. Thank you for supporting the tender keystrokes of a poet, attempting still to make light out of the dark. Thank you for opening yourself up to these other worlds with me. I hope a piece of me somehow stays with you.

Thank you to all of you who have been on my poetry dream team these last ten years, each reader and supporter, each heart in the crowd at open mic, each star in this wide constellation of love. Thank you to: my mother Ester, I love you, mom; my sister Diana, Luis and Alexander; Kahig, Meg and Luca; my inner circle of close ones—you know who you are; my fellow poets out there writing the world back together with your poems; and all the editors of literary journals and magazines who believed in these poems before they became this book. Thank you to Poetry Club. Thank you to my forever first reader, dear friend, and eagle-eyed copyeditor Del Greer. Thank you to Margo McGehee-Kelly, MamaD, Crystal Mercer Watson, and Gin Hartnett for your unwavering love. Thank you to Jane Hirshfield for being my mentor and friend in poems and in spirit. Thank you to every woman I call "Sis" and every man I call "Brother"—you are my tribe of fellow warriors of heart. I love you. I see you.

A deep bow of gratitude to the incredible cast of advanced readers who took these tender poems into their hearts and reflected back such generous blurbs to usher this book into being—Angelique Zobitz, Kimberly Blaeser, Kelli Russell Agodon, CC Mercer Watson, Francesca Bell, and Edward Vidaurre. I am so grateful to you all! And oh my god—the Foreword! Nicole Callihan, I am continuously in awe of you, your poems, your mind, your heart. Thank you for being such a close reader.

Huge thank you to Harbor Editions publisher Allison Blevins for believing so much in this book, and for working with me hand in hand to make it shine. Allison, you are a force of so much good. We are all so thankful for you.

Shout out to my Wednesday Night Poetry family, locally and across the globe virtually, all of you who come in person to Kollective Coffee+Tea in Hot Springs, and all 4,000+ of you who reached your hand out in the dark of the pandemic to touch my hand. It is my honor to hold this space for you, for us. Top-hat tip to Bud Kenny. Thank you Agnes and Kevin Rogers. Thank you poets! *snap, snap*

I have had a lot of organizational support and inspiration that has nourished my art practice the last few years, and I would be remiss if I did not mention the incredible support of everyone at Mid-America Arts Alliance, the Windgate Foundation, the Arkansas Arts Council, Arkansas Learning Through the Arts, Hot Springs National Park, and Diamond Lakes Arkansas Master Naturalists.

Thank you to the more-than-human world—every unique and beautiful species in this book and in my daily life that inspire the unending wonder in me and the fierce desire to protect them. Thank you Genghis and Layla, our beloved Fu dogs and greatest teachers. Thank you trees, air, water, rivers, oceans, bees, butterflies, insects, birds, fish, mammals, sun, wind, whales, rocks, mountains, mosses, deserts, rain, earth. Let my life always be a love letter to you, my heart a sanctuary.

Finally, speaking of sanctuary, my deepest gratitude goes to my wife and love of my life, Joann—the *you* all my love poems are written to; the one who gorgeously paints the covers for my books; the one who has tendered me all these years, from when I was a wild broken thing to the woman I am today. Joann—the one who has lifted all of my veils, broke down all my walls, turned all my doors into windows to let more light in; the one who has built this life beside me, tended the land, fed the birds, protected our wild creatures, filled our home with purpose and love. Joann, the one who also Mothers other kingdoms, other worlds; the one who stirs my spirit to strive toward my truest and highest Self. Joann: you nourish me, you nurture me—you were the first to bring the wild beauty and peace of the natural world to my lips and say *drink*. I love you infinitely.

About the Author

KAI COGGIN (she/her) is the inaugural Poet Laureate of the City of Hot Springs, Arkansas. She is the author of *Mother of Other Kingdoms* and four other collections of poems—*Mining for Stardust* (FlowerSong Press, 2021), *INCANDESCENT* (Sibling Rivalry Press, 2019), *WINGSPAN* (Golden Dragonfly Press, 2016), and *Periscope Heart* (Swimming With Elephants Publications, 2014). Coggin is a Certified Master Naturalist, a K-12 Teaching Artist in poetry with the Arkansas Arts Council, and every week she hosts the longest running consecutive weekly open mic series in the country—Wednesday Night Poetry.

In 2023, Coggin was awarded the CATALYZE grant from the Mid-America Arts Alliance, and the Don Munro Leadership in the Arts Award for Visionary Service. She also received the 2021 Governor's Arts Award for Arts in Education, was twice named "Best Poet in Arkansas" by the *Arkansas Times*, and was nominated for Arkansas State Poet Laureate and Hot Springs Woman of the Year. Her fierce and tender poetry has been nominated six times for The Pushcart Prize, as well as Bettering American Poetry and Best of the Net 2016, 2018, 2021—awarded in 2022. Ten of Kai's poems are going to the moon with the Lunar Codex project, and on earth, they have appeared or are forthcoming in *POETRY, Prairie Schooner, Best of the Net, Cultural Weekly, SOLSTICE, Bellevue Literary Review, The Night Heron Barks, About Place Journal, Lavender Review*, and elsewhere. Coggin is Editor-at-Large at *SWIMM*, Associate Editor at *The Rise Up Review*, and serves on the Board of Directors of the Hot Springs Documentary Film Festival. She lives in a peaceful valley with her wife, where they both tend lovingly to wild ones and each other.

To invite Kai to zoom into your classroom for a reading or workshop, or to have her feature at your literary festival, LGBTQ+ event, school, university, bookclub, or library, please reach out to her at www.kaicoggin.com.

Stay safe, friends. Stay tender.

ABOUT SMALL HARBOR PUBLISHING

Small Harbor Publishing is a 501c3 nonprofit organization. Our goal is to publish unique and diverse voices. We are a feminist press, and we are committed to diversity and inclusion. We strive to fiercely promote the work of our authors and to bring new voices to a devoted and expanding readership.

Small Harbor Publishing began in 2018 with the first issue of *Harbor Review*. The magazine is an online space where poetry and art converse. *Harbor Review* quickly grew and now publishes reviews and runs three micro chapbook competitions, the Washburn Prize, the Editor's Prize, and the Jewish American Woman's Prize.

In July 2020, Small Harbor Publishing was officially incorporated and began Harbor Editions. Harbor Editions accepts submissions through a chapbook open reading period, a hybrid chapbook open reading period, the Marginalia Series, and the Laureate Prize. In 2023, Harbor Anthologies began with a mission to promote texts that explore social justice issues and highlight marginalized writers.

If you would like to support Small Harbor Publishing, please visit our "About" page at https://www.smallharborpublishing.com/about.

Made in the USA
Monee, IL
10 March 2025

13439434R00083